women in
local politics

edited by
debra w. stewart

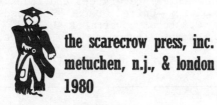
the scarecrow press, inc.
metuchen, n.j., & london
1980

Str. 12.50/6.25/10/x/82

Library of Congress Cataloging in Publication Data

Main entry under title:

Women in local politics.

   Includes bibliographical references and index.
   1. Women in politics--United States--Addresses,
essays, lectures. 2. Local government--United
States--Addresses, essays, lectures. I. Stewart,
Debra W., 1943-
HQ1391.U5W65   305.4'2   80-14526
ISBN 0-8108-1312-2

TABLE OF CONTENTS

v

INTRODUCTION

In recent years growing attention has been paid to the varying political roles women play in the American system. Yet while observers have decried their small numbers, the middle seventies were marked by accelerated female competition for public office. By 1977 the impact of political women on the move stood out in statistics revealing substantial gains in female office holding at all levels across the political system, with the most striking gains emerging at the local level. This introductory essay places local gains in perspective, juxtaposing them to changes on the state and national scene, and considers the implications of such advances in light of the broader literature on female officeholders. In drawing out themes from this existing literature, pathways to power and performance of female incumbents merit special attention.

In the federal system recent gains in female office holding have been markedly skewed toward the executive branch, where women competed favorably for presidential appointment in the Carter administration. By January 1978 women had been tapped for 14 percent of all administration appointments. Two women gained appointment to the federal cabinet, where, before 1977, only three women had ever served. Since 1975 women have not increased their number in two other federal-level institutions, the House of Representatives and the federal judiciary. The eighteen women in the 95th session of the House of Representatives fell one short of their nineteen members serving in the 94th Congress, though the appointment of Muriel Humphrey to office after

3

the death of her husband did introduce one female vote into
the Senate.   Women have also failed to improve their office-
holding status in the federal judiciary.   No woman has ever
served on the Supreme Court.   Only five of the 675 U. S.
Circuit and District Court judges are women.

At the state level women are breaking into the top
executive positions.   By 1978 two governors and three lieutenant governors were women--an increase from 1975, when
one woman served as a governor and one as lieutenant governor.   Gains appear as well in numbers of women occupying
state cabinet-level positions, with an increase from eighty-
four women identified in 1975 to ninety-seven women counted
in 1977.   Currently women occupy about 11 percent of such
posts.   In the state judiciary a modest increase of female
representation is suggested by comparison of the ninety-two
women judges in 1975 to the one hundred ten women in 1977.
Still, women who occupy judgeship on appellate courts and
trial courts of general jurisdiction constitute under 2 percent
of total court membership.   Gains in the state legislature
continue at a steady pace: 101 of the 1, 975 state senators
and 601 of the 5, 583 state representatives were female in
1978.   This count, slightly over 9 percent, advances beyond
the 8 percent benchmark reached in 1975.

Clearly, the most dramatic gains in women's elective
political participation have taken place at the local level.   By
1977 the increase in female local office holding was at least
36 percent above 1975.   In 1975, 5, 931 women held office on
municipal and township governing bodies or in mayoralities,
constituting an estimated 4 percent of officials in offices surveyed.   By 1977 their number had increased to 9, 930, giving
women an estimated 8 percent of total positions.   Even in
county government women are on the move.   In 1975 women
comprised 2 percent (456) of the officials on county governing boards; by 1977 their proportion had increased to 3 percent (660) of the total. [1]

This overview of women in public office evokes at
least three reactions: dismay, that their percentages remain
so small; encouragement, that gradual increases in numbers
are clearly evident; and curiosity, that gains are so heavily
skewed toward the local level.

Common sense and scholarly observation jointly shed
light on this local-strength phenomenon.   Occupying a public
official role at this level is not thought to require quite as

much "role dispensability"[2] as service in other levels of the
system might.   Women serve as public officials in their
home communities; campaign expenditures are more modest
than they might be for higher offices; and women are con-
ventionally thought to be more interested in local, rather
than state or federal, issues. [3]   Still, the local level remains
a relatively unexplored arena for female activism, while researchers set their sights on the more distant national and
state arenas.

        Not withstanding their relatively small numbers, and
perhaps even because of them, women who have gained national elected office have been the subject of considerable
scholarly attention.   Though exceedingly few in number, congresswomen may be the most intensively studied group. [4]
Their meager numbers have necessitated a somewhat episodic
approach to analysis.   In the past few years researchers as
well have learned a great deal about females in the state
houses of the nation. [5]   Since once in state legislative offices
women, unlike men, tend to stay there, and since their proportional representation runs considerably higher in the state
house than in Congress, the state legislatures continue to be
viewed as fertile grounds for research.   In spite of the relative accessibility of local office to women and the fact that
more women are exercising public power at that level than
they are elsewhere, local official participation is the least
studied of the three levels of potential participation within
the federal system.

        This book represents a substantial effort to remedy
this neglect by dealing with two issues central to the analysis
of women in elite roles at the local level.   Those issues are
encapsulated within two questions: how do women attain public office? and, how do women perform once in that public
role?   The first question calls attention to the process of
leadership selection and recruitment; the second evokes concern with policy positions women take and the organizational
roles they assume.

        The discipline of political science as well as the re-
lated fields of social psychology and organization theory provide considerable conceptual development for both sets of
concerns: selection/recruitment and positions/roles.   The
following section explores in light of these broader literatures,
research reporting on political women particularly at the state
and national levels.   The purpose is simply to set the context for a discussion of local level political women.

Selection and Recruitment

What is the nature of the selection process and how has it been found to affect women at other levels of the system? Kenneth Prewitt has characterized the leadership selection generally as a gradual and even process of inclusion and elimination that brings forth from the entire population those few citizens who will hold public office. Prewitt explains:

> Every political community has a comparatively large number of citizens who meet the minimal legal requirements for holding public office. From these citizens come some persons who are attuned to political matters--the politically attentive public. From these comes yet another group which is politically active. And from this group comes an even fewer number of citizens who are actually recruited into the channels which can lead to public office. From these are chosen candidates and from the candidates are chosen a few who will hold public office. [6]

A variety of institutional and individual factors act at each stage of this process to reduce the pool from which office holders will ultimately be drawn. Four dimensions of leadership selection illuminate this weeding-out process.

The first dimension addresses the social bias of leadership and explores the extent to which the leadership group mirrors the demographic characteristics in the population. In comparing the officeholders at all levels in the political system to their respective publics, studies generally find a distinct social bias in leadership selection favoring the dominant socioeconomic strata. [7] Given that this strata is predominantly male, the bias in leadership selection operates to the detriment of female elite participation. While the previous overview of female officeholders did indicate ever-increasing activity among political women, the fact of their dramatic under representation relative to their numbers in the population remains. A focus on the social-bias dimension of leadership selection led the authors of the first comprehensive female officeholder survey to conclude that "the most striking fact about women in political office is that they are so few."[8]

The second dimension of leadership-selection scholar-

ship focuses on political socialization and political mobilization to investigate the likelihood that an individual will enter the group of politically active members of a society from
which leaders are selected. One can be socialized into politics by family or occupation or mobilized into politics by a
worthy cause. In either case the likelihood of eventual office holding is greatly enhanced by the experience.

     The earliest explanation for the limited selection of
women for public service was rooted in this dimension of
leadership-selection scholarship.   Particular focus settled
on socialization and sex-role conditioning. Writing from
this perspective, Robert Lane advanced the proposition that
women are not active in politics generally, because "the
culture emphasizes moral, dependent, and politically less
competent images of women which reduce their partisanship
and sense of political efficacy and define a less active political role for them."[9] Campbell et al. agreed that "the
basic differences that mark the political participation of men
and women we take to lie in vestigial sex roles."[10] Greenstein argued as well for the importance of deeply ingrained
sex roles, identified in childhood, as the key to understanding the sex differential in political activism.[11] Through the
1950s and into the 1960s this was the dominant mode of explanation in the literature on female political participation.

     A third dimension of leadership-selection study turns
to recruitment, probing into both how the individual citizen
decides to aim for a particular office and how political institutions mobilize talent to fill available offices. Here,
questions about the ambition level of potential officeholders
and the paths to public office prescribed by experience of
the predecessor become relevant to determining who will become a viable candidate.

     In recent years students of female participation have
shown increasing interest in this body of theory that suggests
women are blocked from achieving office not merely by socialization but also by situational and structural restraints.
In terms of situational constraints, research tends to indicate that women are less likely to run for office without
their husbands' support.[12] Jeane Kirkpatrick's study of
state legislators found that cooperation from the husband may
be central for women who aspire to public office.[13] In
terms of structural barriers, it is well established that
careers or occupations differ in their capacity to pave the
way for their members to enter public office. Public-office

holders frequently report occupational backgrounds in law
and business, fields where women are thinly scattered.[14]
To the extent that these occupations serve as recruiting
grounds, female opportunity will continue to be restricted
until their numbers in such occupational pools increase.
From the point of view of political institutions responsible
for mobilizing talent for public-office holding, numerous
studies establish the fact that political parties themselves
block women's entry into public office.[15] Recently women's
chances for nomination have increased in what are known
as "throw away districts," report Susan and Martin Tolchin.
In such districts the candidate is expected to lose either because of a strong incumbent, a strong machine, or a combination of both in the opposition forces.[16] Though women
are often recruited as "sacrificial lambs,"[17] Irene Diamond's
findings that a female aspirant's true opportunity to gain state
legislative office is greatest where there is little competition
for seats, reaffirms the central role recruiting institutions
may play in frustrating politically ambitious women.[18]

     A fourth aspect of leadership selection focuses on
campaign strategies selected and ultimate voter choice.
Election studies as such have dominated the landscape of
American political science for several decades. Much of
the literature presents elections as isolated events. But
from the perspective of broad leadership and selection theory, elections and campaigns are merely the final step in
the narrowing process described above. There is only a
modest literature exploring either voter choice or campaign
strategy in elections where a female officeholder is in competition. In terms of strategy, Kirkpatrick reports some
changes at the state legislative level regarding how female
candidates handle their femininity during a campaign: with
perhaps less effort to deny it but still a tendency to ignore
it.[19] As well, Currie, in a case study on her own campaign experience, reports that image and money are particular problems for women campaigners.[20] The CAWP-
Eagleton profile of women holding office offers one of the
few analyses of women experiencing electoral defeat. Sur-
veying women defeated for reelection in 1977, the study
finds that the most-frequently-given reason for electoral defeat was "opposition to women in office." Twenty percent
of the defeated officeholders saw this issue as salient.[21]

Policy Positions and Organizational Roles

     The second set of framing questions for this collec-

tion asks: What difference does it make who occupies
these public offices, either in terms of the policy positions
they take or in terms of the way they organize themselves
for action?   As in the case of leadership selection, more
than one stream of literature contributes to an understanding of these phenomena.   The broader literature on policy
positions assumed by public officials grows out of a more
fundamental concern with the nature of representation; the
literature on internal organization for action, out of analyses
of organizational structure and its relationship to organizational behavior.

Representation in a democracy implies some form of
standing in the place of others--either descriptively, where
the representative constitutes a mirror image of his/her
constituent, or substantively, where representatives stand
for the interests of their constituents.   From a democratic
theory perspective, representation is central, for it is the
mechanism through which citizens have voice in government.
In Part I of this volume we explore the extent to which officeholders are becoming more descriptively representative
of their various publics, specifically through increasing proportions of women among their ranks.   In Part II we turn
to the more difficult issue of substantive representativeness
of female officeholders.

A now-mature literature in empirical political science
both explores a variety of representative styles and considers
the congruence between constituency values and those of the
representative.   Among questions central to this broader
literature are: what personal attitudes about representation
does the official bring to his/her role?   What motivates
his/her actions?   How does the official perceive and interact with the relevant constituency?   The primary thrust of
this research has been toward developing typologies that capture the diversity in representative roles and styles.

The literature focusing on women officeholders already has broadened significantly our understanding of the
nature and substance of official roles.   Studies focusing on
personality traits of women active at the elite level report
that female "politicos" consistently rank higher than male
counterparts on the liberal-conservative scale and display a
greater sense of unconventionality.[22]   At the state level,
where the most extensive work has been completed on roles
and orientations of political women, a number of hypotheses
have been advanced.   Jeane Kirkpatrick concluded from her
study of effective state legislators that women may be more

likely than men to be "problem solvers," concerned with the
substance of policy and legislation and motivated more by a
sense of public duty than by hope of private gain[23] as long
as traditional patterns of value specialization and role distribution are maintained.   In Irene Diamond's study of female state legislators in four New England states, four distinct patterns of adaptation to the legislative environment
were found: "the housewife/benchwarmer," "the traditional
civic worker," "the women's-rights advocate," and "the passive women's-rights advocate"--each reflecting a distinct
conception of what the interests of women are and a sense
of obligation to those interests.[24] Diamond concludes that
the housewife/benchwarmer is incapable of "acting for" any
interest; the traditional civic worker is more capable of influence but not oriented toward "acting for" women; and the
women's-rights advocates--active and passive--do "act for"
women.[25] One conclusion apparent from the research in
this area is that only new categories capture the variation
in the ways women officeholders fulfill the multiple dimensions of their roles.

     The second aspect of this policy-positions/organiza-
tional-roles dimension of women in office asks: what difference does their inclusion in public roles make from an
organizational perspective? Do particular organizational
settings prove more or less conducive to female effectiveness? Does the structure of relationships in which women
public officials are involved influence their behavior and if
so, in what form?

     The organizational-behavior literature, which looks
inside the organization to pinpoint how structural conditions
of organizational life inform organizational behavior, is
most helpful in establishing a framework for discussing
these questions.   Two complementary insights generated by
that literature prove especially useful.   The first suggests
that individuals strive to meet their own needs within the
organization while trying to fulfill the role expectations for
their position.   The second stresses that relationships within organizations are influenced by both intraorganizational
and extraorganizational experiences of persons involved.

     Today a growing body of research on women working
in public and private organizations adapts some of these
more general insights to the study of the relationship between the positions in which women find themselves and their
attitudes and behaviors.   One segment of this literature in-

vestigates the ways in which women function in all-female
voluntary organizations, concluding that by and large they
have provided many women the opportunity to develop leadership and organizational skills that may never have emerged
in "mixed company."[26]

Another very timely strain of research looks at the
impact of sex ratios on the attitudes and behavior of persons in task-oriented groups of various kinds. This literature reports a significant finding that the very situation in
which many women find themselves within organizations--
being in low proportions--may affect them negatively in a
variety of ways. Rosabeth Moss Kanter hypothesizes that
people whose type is represented in very small proportions
in organizations tend to be highly visible and thus under
extraordinary performance pressure. They tend to be isolated from important areas of activity by the "dominants"
in the organization. As well, they tend to find themselves
forced into a narrow range of activities that are consistent
with the dominant group's preconception of their behavior.[27]
Wolman and Frank explore the extreme case of the solo
woman and conclude that the entire peer group containing a
solo woman faces difficult problems. "Its overall produc-
tivity may be lowered by conflict over the woman's role,
and the woman stands a fair chance of becoming a group
casualty."[28]

We noted that the emerging variation in roles political
women play calls forth new analytical categories. Similarly,
new analytical models are necessary to capture the interactions characteristic of those organizational settings within
which these roles are played out. The Kanter and Wolman/
Frank research on interactions in private organizations represents significant steps in that direction.

These introductory comments, presenting an overview
of the literature on attitudes and activities of women in various elite roles, suffices to illustrate the recent mushroom-
ing of interest paralleling the increase in numbers of women
in public office. Many scholars find intriguing the process
of applying theories and concepts developed in various research contexts to the analysis of political women--an activity typically leading to further refinement of existing models. In the present volume Part I focuses on selection and
recruitment, and Part II considers organizational roles and
policy positions. In each case the research spotlights political women who have chosen to develop at least part of their
political careers at the local level.

Notes

        [1]This review of female office holding is based on
the Center for the American Woman and Politics-Eagleton
Institute data-collection effort in this area.   See Marilyn
Johnson with Kathy Stanwick and Lynn Korenblit, Profile of
Women Holding Office (New Brunswick, N.J.: Center for
the American Woman and Politics-Eagleton Institute of Politics, Rutgers University, 1978).
        [2]For a discussion on role pressures reported by
state legislators, see Jeane Kirkpatrick, Political Woman
(New York: Basic Books, 1974), pp. 229-240.
        [3]Albert K. Karnig and B. Olive Walter, "Election
of Women to City Councils," Social Science Quarterly 56,
4 (March 1976):   605-613.
        [4]Emmy Werner, "Women in Congress," Western
Political Quarterly 19 (March 1966):   16-30; Morrigene Hol-
comb, "Women in the U.S. Congress," rev. ed. (Washington, D.C.: Congressional Research Service, Library of
Congress, April 21, 1971); Charles S. Bullock, III, and
Patricia Lee Findley Heys, "Recruitment of Women for
Congress: A Research Note," Western Political Quarterly
25 (September 1972):   416-423; Hope Chamberlain, A Minor-
ity of Members: Women in the U.S. Congress (New York:
Praeger, 1973); Freida L. Gehlen, "Women in Politics,"
in Walter D. Burnham, ed., Politics/America (New York:
Van Nostrand, 1973, pp. 181-186); Susan Tolchin, Women
in Congress (Washington, D.C.: Government Printing Of-
fice, 1976); and R. Darcy and Sarah Slavin Schramm, "When
Women Run Against Men," Public Opinion Quarterly 41
(Spring 1977):   1-14.
        [5]See especially Kirkpatrick, Political Woman, and
Irene Diamond, Sex Roles in the State House (New Haven:
Yale University Press, 1977).
        [6]Kenneth Prewitt, The Recruitment of Political Lead-
ers: A Study of Citizen Participation (Indianapolis: Bobbs-
Merrill, 1970), p. 7.
        [7]Ibid., p. 206.
        [8]Johnson with Stanwick and Korenblit, Profile of
Women Holding Office, p. xx.
        [9]Robert Lane, Political Life (New York: Free Press,
1959), p. 215.
        [10]Angus Campbell et al., The American Voter (New
York: John Wiley, 1964), p. 484.
        [11]Fred Greenstein, Children and Politics (New Haven:
Yale University Press, 1969), pp. 118-127.
        [12]Emily Stoper, "Wife and Politician: Role Strain

Among Women in Public Office," in Marianne Githens and
Jewel L. Prestage, A Portrait of Marginality: The Political
Behavior of the American Woman (New York: David McKay,
1977).

13Kirkpatrick, Political Woman, p. 231.

14The legal profession in particular serves as recruiting grounds for state legislatures. Jewell and Patterson report that since 1900 nearly one-quarter of legislators
have been lawyers. Malcolm Jewell and Samuel C. Patterson, The Legislative Process in the U.S. (New York: Random House, 1973), p. 75.

15Peggy Lamson, Few Are Chosen: American Women
in Political Life Today (Boston: Houghton Mifflin, 1960); and
Kirsten Amundsen, The Silenced Majority (Englewood Cliffs,
N.J.: Prentice-Hall, 1971).

16Susan Tolchin and Martin Tolchin, Clout: Womanpower and Politics (New York: Capricorn Books, 1976), p.
68.

17Susan Carroll, "Women Candidates and State Legislative Elections, 1976: Limitations on the Political Opportunity Structure and Their Effects on Electoral Participation and Success," paper prepared for Annual Meeting of
American Political Science Association, Washington, D.C.,
1977, p. 23.

18Diamond, Sex Roles in the State House.

19Kirkpatrick, Political Woman, pp. 99-103.

20Virginia Currey, "Campaign Theory and Practice--
The Gender Variable," in Githens and Prestage, A Portrait
of Marginality, pp. 139-149.

21Marilyn Johnson and Susan Carroll, Profile of
Women Holding Office II (New Brunswick, N.J.: Center for
the Woman and Politics-Eagleton Institute of Politics, Rutgers University, 1978).

22See Emmy E. Werner and Louise M. Bachtold,
"Personality Characteristics of Women in American Politics,"
in Jane Jaquette, ed., Women in Politics (New York: John
Wiley and Sons, 1974); Emmy Werner, "Women in State Legislatures," Western Political Quarterly 21 (1968): 40-50;
and Marie Rosenberg, "Political Efficacy and Sex Roles:
Congresswomen Hansen and Green," paper presented to the
Annual Meeting of the American Political Science Association, Washington, D.C., September 1972.

23Kirkpatrick, Political Woman, p. 211.

24Diamond, Sex Roles in the State House, p. 162.

25Ibid., pp. 116-164.

26Martin Gruberg, Women in American Politics (Oshkosh, Wis.: Academia Press, 1968), p. 116.

[27]Rosabeth Moss Kanter, "Some Effects of Proportions on Group Life: Skewed Ratios and Response to Token Women," American Journal of Sociology 82 (March 1977): 965-970.

[28]Carol Wolman and Hal Frank, "The Solo Woman in a Professional Peer Group," in Harold H. Frank, Women in the Organization (Philadelphia: University of Pennsylvania Press, 1977), p. 254.

PART I

Selection and Recruitment of Women:
Pathways to Local Office

Prompted by a vision of democracy placing a premium on ever-expanding citizen involvement in government, many observers of American local politics advocate increased participation of women in public-office holding. Yet in pursuing strategies toward that goal, the question of which factors actually constrain or enhance the opportunity structure for women becomes central. The narrowing process through which the mass public is reduced to those for whom office-holding is a likely possibility obviously affects men and women differently. The research presented in this section aims to increase our understanding of how that process affects specifically female pathways to public power.

Several factors influencing the routes women take to public office emerge as salient. Practices of the political institutions through which many aspiring officials serve out their "apprenticeship" command early attention. How do political parties facilitate the passage of women from party activists to officeholders? Do they offer equal training opportunities to members of both sexes? What implications might party practices hold for female office holding at the local level?

A second set of questions concerns the attitudinal context within which selection and recruitment take place. We generally assume that different social political contexts, sometimes labeled political cultures, are more receptive to women in public roles than are others. Yet to date little research actually testing hypotheses about the likely direc- tion of the impact of different political cultures on female opportunity structure has been completed. Thus, we are prompted to ask: how do differences in the social political context expand or contract opportunity for female office hold- ing?

A third set of questions focuses on the socialization patterns of women as contrasted to men who attain public office. Do the patterns differ, and if so, how? How im- portant is socialization as compared to family situation or occupational qualifications in balancing barriers to female office holding?

Finally, a fourth group of questions probes the dif- ference between actual pathways to power pursued by men and women. Do the same kinds of experiences ease the way to power for females and males alike, or have females built a recruitment road unique to the life situation of the traditional women?

Answers to the broad question "Who achieves po- litical office and how do they get there?" will emerge from pursuing each of these sets of questions in a variety of of- ficial contexts. The four articles in Part I reflect recent research aimed at answering these questions in terms of those offices available to women on the local level. The first paper considers available apprenticeship experiences for women in the political parties. The second paper ex- amines the impact of political culture on the opportunity for women to attain seats on trial-court benches. Two addition- al papers focus on local elected council members. One of the papers considers council members in suburban munici- palities surrounding Chicago. In the other paper a random sample of female representatives on local Connecticut legis- lative bodies, with a matched sample of male officeholders, forms the data base for analysis.

In "The Invisible Hands: Sex Roles and the Division of Labor in Two Local Political Parties," Diane Margolis studies the division of labor between men and women in the Democratic and Republican party organizations of a small New England town. Previous research would lead us to conclude that there exists a sex-linked difference in such apprenticeship activity. In the Margolis work, interviews, observations, and logs kept by town committee members re-

veal a difference in styles of performance that makes men
stand out more than women. Women's political activities
more often took place in settings where they could not be
seen, and the roles played by women were typically those
without title or acknowledgment while men usually held highly visible leadership positions. Margolis finds a similarity
between sex-linked roles and behavior patterns based in the
family and the parts played in the political arena. Because
of these differences, women often were unnoticed and unre-
warded, although more than twice the amount of time spent
on political activities during the study period were women
hours, and women logged more than three times as many
separate political interactions as men.

Beverly Cook in her article "Political Culture and
Selection of Women Judges in Trial Courts" looks at the
impact of political culture on the opportunity structure of
females to attain judicial posts. Working with Daniel Elazar's notion of political culture, which categorizes political
systems according to their dominant political culture, be it
moralistic, individualistic, or traditional, Cook finds that
the distribution of female judges fits her prediction. There
are twice as many women judges on the appellate level in
the moralistic as in the individualistic or traditionalist
states and more than twice as many as on the minor-court
level. She does find, however, that differences appear less
important on the general-jurisdiction trial courts, with fifty-
nine women judges in the moralistic states, forty-four in
the individualistic states, and thirty-one in the traditional
states. In general, the political-culture variable is useful
in understanding that women are admitted to the political
system as judicial authorities in accord with structural, attitudinal, and behavioral features of the subculture. The
percentage allowed to participate where barriers have been
broken may depend upon the percentage of women with the
social and legal credentials.

In "The Effects of Sex on Recruitment: Connecticut
Local Offices," Susan Gluck Mezey examines political recruitment and socialization patterns of men and women local
office holders in Connecticut. Socialization, situational, and
structural differences between males and females in this
sample were barely apparent. Although the women were
somewhat educationally and socially disadvantaged compared
to the men with whom they served, this disadvantage did
not carry great weight in local office. Connecticut women,
for example, were not subject to greater family constraints,

nor were they subject to harassment from voters because
of sex discrimination. The greatest background difference
between male and female officeholders appeared in their occupations, with one-third of the women coming to local office as housewives. As well, a major difference between
male and female politicians in Connecticut appeared in their
political-party backgrounds, with women more frequently engaged in party work before election to office. Still, most
sex differences in recruitment that had been found at other
levels of office were not evident among Connecticut local
politicians.

     The article by Sharyne Merritt, "Recruitment of
Women to Suburban City Councils: Higgins vs. Chevalier,"
explores the question, "Do the resources and backgrounds of
women in local politics more closely approximate the Henry
Higgins ideal of 'a woman being more like a man' or Maurice Chevalier's model of gender-related difference?" Three
hypotheses emerge as salient within the context of this general question. Hypothesis 1 would suggest that while male
and female elites share some common personality traits,
women lack characteristics that may be necessary for political advancement at the local level. Hypothesis 2 suggests
that women are constrained by social roles and lack of social resources. Hypothesis 3 would suggest that women are
like men: male and female local elites follow similar paths
to politics. In terms of personality traits, Merritt finds
evidence to support both the Higgins and the Chevalier positions. While there are no sex differences in motivation,
sex differences do appear in social resources and roles, although with reservation. On recruitment, the Higgins posi-
tion--that is, women and men are essentially similar--draws
substantial support. There are not sex differences in the
years of residence, the recruiting agent, appointment, or
participation in church, service, nonpartisan or partisan
groups across sex. Considering ambition differences among
local officials provides additional insight into the impact of
sex. Among the ambitious, men and women are similar in
personality traits and perception of role conflicts, but will
follow different recruitment paths. Sex differences in personality and roles and sex similarities in recruitment seem
to apply largely to those local officeholders who are not
ambitious for higher office.

     The findings presented in Part I shed significant
light on our understanding of leadership and selection processes for female public-office holders. Some findings

confirm the reports of earlier studies; others contradict
generally accepted hypotheses; and still others break new
ground in relatively unexplored areas.   The influence wield-
ed by political culture and activities within local political
parties to shape the opportunity structure for female aspirants is clearly portrayed in the Cook and Margolis studies.
Similarly confirming are the Mezey and Merritt reports that
most women bring to their activist role fewer social resources than do their male counterparts.   Yet Mezey's other
finding of few sex differences in socialization or situation of
Connecticut local-office holders does represent somewhat of
a departure from the general formulation emerging from
earlier work in the area.   It may be that the very nature
of local office is qualitatively different from offices at other
levels.   Only future research will clarify this point.   However, Merritt's suggestion that differences between men and
women officcholders across the board might fall out entirely
when focusing only on ambitious women, highlights a new variable that should be entered into the explanation equation in
all future leadership studies of women.

THE INVISIBLE HANDS: SEX ROLES AND THE DIVISION OF LABOR IN TWO LOCAL POLITICAL PARTIES

Diane Margolis

Women make up a majority of the U.S. electorate, yet they hold few high-ranking positions in government. Classic studies of the American political system, if they mention women at all, generally limit their analyses to a note on the insignificance of women's participation.[1] Recently the women's movement has turned attention to women's role in politics, and several reports have been published.[2] Most of these, however, concentrate on the few women who do achieve political standing, overlooking the many who take the first step beyond the ballot box into their local political organization but who seldom advance further. Yet it is at the base of the political system, in the local organization, that many political careers are spawned while others are aborted.[3] We know little about what happens to women there.

The objective of this paper is to begin to fill this gap. It is based on a study that, by examining in detail the day-to-day workings of two local political organizations, seeks to bring out the social patterns and interpersonal behaviors that might help reveal the process by which equality at the base of the political system yields to increasing inequalities as political hierarchies are ascended.

22

Background and Methods

The thirteen female and twenty-three male respondents were the members of the Republican and Democratic
Town Committees of Fairtown, Connecticut. [4] In Connecticut, as in most other New England states, affairs of both
political parties are conducted at the grassroots level by
Town Committees.   These bodies serve as a kind of personnel department for their towns.   They interview and
recommend candidates for appointive offices and they en-
dorse candidates for elective offices.   In addition, they run
local political campaigns, serve as links to the state party
organizations, and determine the local party's position on
issues.

Fairtown is an affluent, almost entirely (98.9 percent)
white community of about 18,000.   In 1970 the median years
of education for Fairtowners was thirteen; the median family
income was close to $17,000; almost 60 percent of the em-
ployed men (only 1.6 percent of the men were unemployed)
worked as professionals, technicians, managers, or propri-
etors; and over half of them worked out of town.   Of the
10,000 voters registered in 1973, more than half were registered Republicans, the rest splitting almost evenly between
Democrats and unaffiliated voters.   The actual political di-
visions, however, were more complicated.   Both parties
were split between conservative and liberal or moderate factions, the latter having gained a bare majority on both party's
Town Committees shortly before the study began.

The group under study was small and not statistically
representative of the American population, nor even of grass-
roots political organizations, and therefore generalizations
must be made with caution.   Nevertheless, because the focus was on those ordinary, taken-for-granted acts that are
part of the everyday fabric of our culture, intensive and
microscopic data-collection techniques, impossible to perform with large samples, were necessary.

Members of the two Town Committees were interviewed frequently and observed at meetings and other political gatherings from September through December 1974.
In addition, at the initial interview each respondent was giv-
en a form on which to record all his/her political activities
each week.   Although each committee member was asked to
record all conversations that had any political content, and
all the work each subject had done for the party, there were

Chart 1

Sample Log   Name   Male

NAME OF CONTACT	T	SITE	SUBJECT, CONCLUSIONS, COMMENTS	TIME
Democratic	1	Phone	Listened to local and state candidates give speeches at opening of headquarters. Signed roster to work at P. H. on October 26.	20 min.
Candidate for State Assembly	2	Phone	Urged H. to attend seminar on energy at church in order to share his knowledge, gain insights, and present himself to a portion of the electorate that rarely sees local candidates first-hand.	5 min.
Candidate for State Senate	3	Phone	Sought his headquarters phone pursuant to inviting him to the energy seminar.	5 min.
J. N. K. S.	4	Party	Discussed candidacy of P. for Probate Judge; said I had offered to bring P. through C. area.	10 min.
Church Congregation	5	Church	Encouraged nonregistered to register to vote; encouraged attendance at upcoming meeting of housing authority.	10 min.
Townspeople	6	School Auditorium	Attended meeting on housing authority.	2 hrs.
Church Congregation	7	Church	Participated in discussion of crisis (population, food, energy) facing mankind; discussed importance of knowing legislator's stand on these issues.	$1\frac{1}{2}$ hrs.
Tenants	8	C. Apartment	Distributed circular encouraging non-registered tenants to register to vote on this their last opportunity before the November election. More than 10 eventually registered.	

			Sample Log	Name Female

NAME OF CONTACT	T	SITE	SUBJECT, CONCLUSIONS, COMMENTS	TIME
J.	1	Phone	Press release--B.'s addresses.	20 min.
P.	2	Phone	Campaign 10/3 meeting.	$\frac{1}{2}$ hour
B.	3	Phone	J.'s calendar and press release.	45 min.
S.	4	Phone	Ad's, Ballots, Meeting H.Q. 10 a.m.	$\frac{1}{2}$ hour
M.	5	Phone	P. scooped us on format for Ad.	5 min.
Campaign Staff	6	House	Layout ads, appearances, newspaper releases, etc.	$2\frac{1}{2}$ hrs.
W.	7	Phone	Re: R.'s Coffee.	20 min.
A.	8	Phone	H.W. opening.	5 min.
A.	9	Phone	T.C. Square Dance.	20 min.
J.	10	Phone	Absentee ballot and letter insert.	5 min.
M.	11	Phone	Ads for J.	10 min.
S.	12	Phone	Absentee ballots.	5 min.
J.	13	Phone	Absentee ballots, Ads, T.	15 min.
J.	14	Phone	Absentee ballots.	3 min.
J.	15	Phone	Absentee ballots.	5 min.
A.	16	Phone	T.C. Square Dance re: status and food.	10 min.
M.	17	Phone	Why and How Politics--AAUW --press releases.	10 min.
M.	18	M.'s House	Writing ads, reception of Teen Center, supporting other candidates next election.	
J.	19	Phone	Absentee ballot re: talk Teen Center.	
S.	20	Phone	Reaction to her article in Press.	
M.H.	21	Phone	Reaction to S.'s article.	
M.	22	Phone	J.'s article.	
Town Council Meeting	23	H.Q.	Campaign support for candidate.	

variations in the completeness of the logs. In general, the
men were slightly better log keepers than the women. This
would have tended to exaggerate the amount of activity of
the males and minimized that of the females, a possible
bias in a direction opposite from the findings. Thus, differences between the men and women might have been ob-
scured but none was likely to be introduced by uneven log
keeping.

Amount and Location of Activity

Men outnumbered women on both Town Committees--
thirteen to six on the Republican Town Committee and ten
to seven on the Democratic Town Committee--but the women
were far more active than the men. Of the 1,832 interactions recorded, 1,185, or about two-thirds, were performed by women. The average number of interactions per
man was thirty-one, while the average for the women was
three times that, or one hundred. This was an unexpected
finding, because men had seemed to be as frequently present
as women at meetings, fund-raisers, and work sessions.

The location of their activities helps explain why
women seemed less busy than they actually were. Whatever the men and women were doing politically could range
from the highly noticeable to the invisible. Public speeches
were probably the most noticeable activity, while work done
alone was the least noticed. In between were attendance at
meetings, fund-raisers, or group work sessions at which
one would be seen by several others; or phone conversations,
which would be noticed by only one other. Women's activities tended to take place in situations where they would not
be widely observed; the reverse was true of men's activities.

Both men and women did a lot of telephoning, but a
greater percentage of women's interactions, 51 percent, took
place over the phone as against 42 percent of men's interactions. Moreover, although such tasks as setting up fund-
raisers or preparing mailing accounted for about the same
proportion, 15 percent, of men's and women's activities,
women were more likely to work alone. Solitary work made
up 43 percent of women's and 35 percent of men's work.
Face-to-face encounters, which included meetings that were
likely to be group sessions and other situations where participants would be noticed by many others, accounted for 43 percent of the items reported by men and 34 percent of those
reported by women.

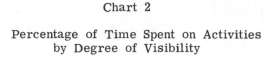

Chart 2

Percentage of Time Spent on Activities
by Degree of Visibility

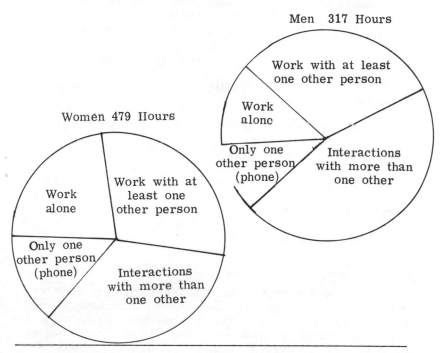

Men   317 Hours

Work with at least
one other person

Work
alone

Only one
other person
(phone)

Interactions
with more than
one other

Women 479 Hours

Work
alone

Work with at
least one
other person

Only one
other person
(phone)

Interactions
with more than
one other

Another way to examine the relative invisibility of
women's political activities is to consider the amount of
time spent on different kinds of activities.   Apparently,
women were spending less time per item than men--the
difference between them in time spent was not as great as
the difference in the number of separate items reported.
Of the 796 hours spent on politics by Town Committee members, 479, or 60 percent, were woman-hours as opposed
to 317, or 40 percent, man-hours.   In the pie-chart (Chart
2) the shaded areas represent high-visibility activity, the
cross-hatched areas limited-visibility activity, and the
white areas hidden activities, i.e., solitary work.   Plain-
ly, women were spending a far greater percentage of their
time in hidden or limited-visibility activity than were the
men, close to half of whose activity was highly visible.

Social Networks

Table 1

Percentage of Interactions with Persons of Same Gender
Within and Outside
Own Town Committee by Recorder's Gender

Recorder's Gender

	Female	Male
Same Gender		
Our Town Committee	55.7%	48.1
base	(228)	(208)
Same Gender Outside	72.4%	63.2%
Our Town Committee		
base	(239)	(155)

Although women were more likely to work alone or
with just one other person, the range of their associations
was greater than men's. Women's communications were
not as restricted to members of their Town Committees as
were men's. Forty-nine percent of women's interactions
were within their own Town Committees as opposed to 58
percent of men's. Moreover, the average woman interac-
ted with a greater number of other persons (eighteen) than
the average man (ten). On the other hand, especially when
venturing beyond their own Town Committees, women were
much more likely than men to restrict their interactions to
persons of their own gender. Clearly then, all members of
the Town Committees were parochial, interacting almost exclusively with others of their own party, if not necessarily
with their Town Committee colleagues, and predominantly
with persons of their own gender; but men showed a somewhat greater tendency to be ideocentric--restricting their
interactions to persons of the same political persuasion--
while women showed a greater tendency towards sexocen-
trism--restricting their communications more to persons of
the same gender.

Topics of Talk and Kinds of Work

What were all those communications about? When
we look at the subjects that men and women discussed and
the tasks they worked on, patterns emerged that further explain the invisibility of women and also indicate differences
in the roles men and women assumed. Table 2 summarizes
the information on subjects.

Table 2

Subject of Interaction by Recorder's Gender

Subject	Recorder's Gender		Percent of All Items in This Category
	Female	Male	
Women's Talk	74.6 (753)	25.4 (256)	59.4
Women's Work I	76.9 (143)	23.1 (43)	10.9
Women's Work II	46.6 (62)	53.4 (71)	7.8
Androgynous Talk	38.5 (79)	61.5 (126)	12.1
Androgynous Work	40.6 (13)	59.4 (19)	1.9
Men's Talk	25.8 (16)	74.2 (46)	3.6
Men's Work	23.3 (17)	76.7 (56)	4.3

In the initial coding, ninety-nine separate subject categories
were used. A few were: "attending a Town Committee
Meeting," "discussing the campaign," "seeking advice,"
"getting information," "giving information," and "discussing
a political issue." Then the subjects were grouped into

three categories: those engaged in more by women; those
participated in about equally by men and women; and those
dominated by men. Because there were twice as many men
as women, only those categories that were recorded more
than twice as often by men were included in "Men's Talk"
and "Men's Work"; those categories in which men recorded
items about twice as often as women were listed under "Androgynous Talk" and "Androgynous Work"; and the kinds of
work and talk that were listed at least twice as often by
women as by men were listed under "Women's Talk" and
"Women's Work."

Women's Talk

        Women's Talk most often involved an exchange of in-
formation. When an extra meeting was called or when the
time or place of a regular meeting was changed, women
would spread that information. (See items two, four, seven,
and eight on the woman's sample log, Chart 1.) If facts
had to be gathered, such as the rulings on absentee ballots,
a woman would call some authority to find out. Not infre-
quently, if a man needed some information he would ask a
woman to get it for him. (See items thirteen through fifteen: Joe, a candidate, asked the log keeper to get information about absentee ballots from Janet, the Town Clerk.)

        Women also talked about arrangements for work tasks.
Whether it was a mailing that had to be sent out, a fund-
raiser that had to be set up, or some other task, women
were almost invariably the ones who took upon themselves
the responsibility of organization and management. They
usually did this in committees or teams, and sometimes
men were included. Profuse communications were generated in the coordination of every task and it often took far
more separate interactions, if not more time, to get any
job set up than it took to actually do the work. (Note, for
instance, on the sample female log that it took six communications to arrange for absentee ballots to be sent to voters.)

        Third, women talked--mostly among themselves, but
sometimes with men--about the campaign. When a candidate
issued a statement, or a speech was made, or some decision was needed about how to run a campaign, women sought
out each other's opinion; and they discussed and analyzed
the virtues and shortcomings of candidates and their cam-
paigns--frequently and at some length. (See items seventeen,

eighteen, twenty, and twenty-one on the sample female
log.)

The fourth most common topic of Women's Talk was
problems on their own Town Committees.

Finally, women more often than men ranged from
one topic to another.   For example, nine of the twenty-two
items on the woman's sample log covered more than one
subject.

Men's Talk

The most common item on the men's logs was an
attempt to influence another person.   (See items two, five,
seven, and eight on the male sample log.)   Most Male Talk
about specific issues took place just before a vote was sched-
uled.   Women's talk about most topics, even those on which
a vote was eventually held, was usually spread over a pro-
tracted period before the issue came to a decision.

In addition to conversations aimed at influencing
others, men's logs included more mentions of large-group
functions at which attendance would be noticed by many
others--parties, fund-raisers, rallies, and openings of campaign headquarters.

Androgynous Talk

Some activities would be required of any Town Committee member, and these appeared equally in men's and
women's logs.   Meetings were well attended, although there
were a few persons on both Town Committees who seldom
showed up.   They were as likely to be women as men.
Sometimes those who came to the Town Committee seeking
to be nominated or recommended for positions would call
Town Committee members before the meeting.   Because
candidates for appointment usually made sure to canvass
all members, the men on the Town Committees were as
likely to be called as the women.   Also, when a Town
Committee member wished assistance in some task, such
as election-day calling, he or she--it was usually a "she"
because most arrangements were made by women--would
often call all the members of her own Town Committee before looking outside for help.   Before the meetings at which

Town Committee vacancies were filled, a large number of
intrafaction communications were necessary in order to sew
up the votes.   Again, these calls were as likely to be received by men as by women.

Women's Work

        Women's Work mostly involved fund-raisers and
mailings.   Women would write the material for mailings,
arrange to have it printed, get voters lists from the regis-
trar of voters, and divide up the list among those who were
to address the envelopes.   Once, in order to spread the
work more evenly, the Republicans set aside a special Town
Committee meeting for the addressing of envelopes, but
even then all the preparatory work was done by women.
Mailings sent out by the Democratic party were addressed
at home, alone, by women.   In addition to the mailings,
preparation of food for fund-raisers accounted for most of
the solitary work done by women.

        Another task performed almost exclusively by women
was pickups and deliveries.   News releases, which had to
be seen by several members of the Town Committee before
they were submitted to the paper, were passed from one
person to another by female couriers, and deposits that had
to be made at the bank were also handled by women.

        It has been suggested[5] that women devote more time
to political tasks because they do not have the career responsibilities that men do.   This study did not bear that
out.   A majority of the women worked outside the home at
least part-time or had preschool children.

        Another explanation of women's greater contribution
could be that their other activities did not take them out of
town while many of the men's jobs did.   Yet even on week-
ends women were busier at politics than men.

        One common assumption is that men but not women
receive help from their spouses--a situation that should give
the men an advantage, making them appear to be harder-
working than they actually are.   To check this view, I asked
members to include in their logs any political work their
spouses did.   As it turned out, half the assumption proved
correct--women did receive virtually no assistance from
their husbands; but, surprisingly, few of the men were

helped by their spouses either. Only three of the men, all
of them on the Republican Town Committee, had wives who
gave significant assistance.

Men's Work

        In addition to the group-work sessions in which men
participated somewhat more than women, Men's Work included responsibilities as Republican Box Captains and work
with the party clubs. Although the men who had led the
moderate Republican Club and the liberal Democratic Club
gave up their official positions on those clubs after they be-
came members of the Town Committees, they continued to
maintain an active interest in the clubs.

Androgynous Work

        Androgynous Work included tasks done by the Town
Committee officials--mostly preparing reports for meetings--
and setting up and attending coffees at which candidates met
voters. Because official positions and subcommittee chair-
personships were divided between men and women in rough
proportion to their membership on the Town Committees, report preparation was also divided. Androgynous Work, however, accounted for only 2 percent of the activities that were
recorded.

        To summarize: The subjects women talked about
tended to be general and far-ranging, and they often covered
several topics in a single conversation. Commonly when
women wished a change of some sort they casually initiated
issues to test for support. Men's Talk, on the other hand,
covered just a single subject; normally it arose at the mo-
ment when some issue was about to be decided; and generally it had a specific goal--to garner support for some position. Where women's talk was specific, it had as its goal
not so much the influencing of another as an exchange of information or the organization of a work task.

        Women took care of what needed to be done for the
day-to-day maintenance of the Town Committees. Tasks
that normally must be done on a regular monthly or yearly
basis were more likely to be undertaken by women, especially if those chores were not attached to an official role. In
contrast, men did only that work that was assigned to them

by virtue of the official positions they held, and whatever
they did beyond that was usually a special or nonrecurring
job. Women worked behind the scene; men worked in public.

The Unofficial Roles Women Play

        Up until now items in the logs have been grouped by
gender as if all the men and all the women contributed equally to the work and talk of their parties. They didn't. Some
men and some women were hardly doing a thing while others
were working and talking prodigiously. In fact, thirteen
men, more than two-thirds of the men who were keeping
logs, 6 recorded less than forty interactions; three recorded
between forty and sixty; and another three between sixty and
one hundred. No man recorded more than one hundred interactions. The balance shifts in the opposite direction on
the distaff side. Four women recorded more than one hundred interactions; one logged between sixty and one hundred;
three between forty and fifty-nine; and three others logged
fewer than forty.

        What accounts for these differences in activity? With-
out exception those who recorded more than forty interactions were playing a special role. There was, however, a
strategic difference between the roles played by men and
those played by women. Only men who had titular status
recorded more than fifty interactions, while most of the
roles women played were parts without title or acknowledgment.

        Party chairpersons were the most active men. The
Republican logged eighty-two interactions and the Democrat
sixty-seven. The Republican treasurer, a man, logged precisely the same number, fifty-two, as his Democratic counterpart, a woman. Two other men logging more than forty
interactions were the former chairpersons of the party clubs.
They continued to lead their factions after they were elected
to the Town Committee by assuming the unofficial role of
"Advisor-to-the-Majority." The sixth man with more than
forty interactions was a Republican who assisted his party's
Advisor-to-the-Majority.

        All other unofficial roles were played by women. 7
There was no regular position for a person who would spread
news throughout the Town Committee and keep the Committee
in touch with other groups in town, and yet both parties had

such a woman, whom we shall call the "Communicator-in-
Chief." As has already been noted, there was a great deal
of routine work especially related to getting out the vote and
raising money that by unwritten rule was to have been shared
equally by all the Town Committee members. It wasn't.
Each Town Committee had a woman, whom we shall call the
"Drudge," who assumed much of that burden. Again, when
a Town Committee vote was nearing, someone had to call
members to make sure they attended the meeting and voted
with their faction. Only the moderate Republicans and liberal Democrats seemed to have such a person, a woman, whom
we shall call the "Majority Whip." But the Majority Whip
did not decide how her faction should act; for that she turned
to the man we call the Advisor-to-the-Majority. Most notable was the fact that, different as the parties were, almost
identical roles appeared in both, and the gender of the persons filling parallel roles was the same in both parties.

The Communicator-in-Chief

The role that called for the most interactions was
that of Communicator-in-Chief. It was played on the Republican Town Committee by Sophie Morelli, and on the
Democratic Town Committee by Janie Brown. They acted
as intermediaries between the factions in their parties; carried information and other communications between the Town
Committee and other groups in town; and even on occasion
linked the two Town Committees. Although her political activities were extensive, they were but a small part of the
Communicator-in-Chief's community participation--she was
active in several organizations, and this brought her into
acquaintanceships with persons all over town.

Sophie Morelli, an eighty-year-old woman who had
been active in Fairtown's Republican party for close to a
half-century, ambled through Town Hall each day having a
word with her relatives (a daughter and a grandchild) and
others who worked there, picking up and spreading bits and
pieces of the news of the day. She often lunched at a local
diner, the clientele of which was made up mostly of conservative Republicans. They interspersed gossip about wed-
dings, births, children, and divorces with discussion of candidates and political issues. When there was an important
development, Morelli would call her party chairperson. Whatever there was to say, she talked with several members of
her Town Committee daily.

Although Janie Brown was clearly a liberal Democrat, she worked hard to maintain her ties in other groups. Her town chairperson, a conservative, spoke with her more than with anyone else in the liberal faction. Indeed, of all the members on both Town Committees, Janie Brown was the one with the broadest network of contacts. The average woman on a Town Committee talked with only twenty other persons; in Brown's log there was mention of almost twice that number, thirty-eight.

Majority Whip

To get out the faction's vote there was in each majority faction a Whip. The Majority Whip usually notified the Advisor-to-the-Majority when concerted action was needed and then, after she and the Advisor had decided what was to be done, called others in their faction. Before an important vote was taken, Barbara Weatherton conferred with her two Advisors-to-the-Majority and then canvassed the moderates.

Several times during that autumn the liberal Democrats decided to caucus. When they did they usually met at Marjorie Hastings' house, and it was she who called the others to the meeting. Many additional meetings were also held at her house; it was usually she who acted as the unofficial moderator. The Whip had two other functions. If a position was open and no one to the liking of the faction came forward, the Whip would try to find a candidate. (In the Democratic party Hastings shared this job with Brown.) She also filled in whenever a male failed to carry out his assignment. For instance, the Democratic campaign manager took a trip to Europe two weeks before the election: Hastings then ran the campaign.

The role of Whip involved a large number of communications. Hastings listed one hundred twenty-one interactions with thirty-two different persons, and she was listed in other persons' logs forty-nine times. Weatherton was somewhat less active; she listed eighty-two separate interactions with twenty-six different persons and was mentioned in the logs of others only seven times.

The Drudges

Another unofficial role that involved many interactions

and was performed exclusively by women was that of Drudge.
The Drudge made most of the arrangements for fund-raisers;
prepared more than her share of the food; decorated the
room in which the fund-raisers were held; cleaned up after-
wards; made arrangements for mailings and addressed more
envelopes than anyone else.   Unlike others on the Town Committee, a large percentage of the Drudge's work was done
alone.   Edna Halsey, the Democratic Drudge, logged a modest forty-six items, but for 36 percent of those items she
was working alone preparing food, ironing tablecloths for a
fund-raiser square dance, and addressing envelopes.   The
Republican Drudge was Mary Kelley.   Her log does not show
such a high percentage of work done alone because she was
also an assistant Communicator-in-Chief for Morelli.   Besides, the Republican treasury was ample, so most of their
fund-raisers were catered, requiring many arrangements
but not much solitary preparation.

Mary Kelley and Edna Halsey handled the role of
Drudge differently.   Halsey was assigned tasks by other
women who organized the affairs at which she worked.   Kelley was self-directed.   She organized the tasks and tried to
get others to help out, but then did most of the work herself.   Both women were appreciated for what they did, but
only Kelley was respected for it.   A number of Republican
men lauded her with the same words: "What we need in
this party is more women like Kelley."   And Kelley, fully
a year before nominations were in order, was being urged
to run for selectperson or even for "First."

Edna Halsey was strictly a Drudge.   A feminist Democratic woman said of her: "I don't know why she was ever
put on that Town Committee.   She's a sweet lady, she does
all the cooking and baking and fussing at parties, but political philosophy is beyond her."

Conclusions

Women who enter politics tend to be motivated either
by a service orientation or by what Daniel Elazar has called
a "moralistic" political orientation--belief that politics is
"one of the great activities of man in his search for the
good society."[8]   The service orientation lends itself to the
role of Drudge, and women who view politics as a locale
for giving are welcome in any political party.   The Idealistic orientation is not so welcome.   Women who view politics
as an opportunity to help bring forth a better world are likely

to find their way into politics only where the system is
open.   Politics in Fairtown was open, but not so open that
individuals filled roles by virtue of their talents rather than
their gender.

        This is, of course, not the first time a study has
uncovered unofficial division of labor by gender where the
rules called for equality.   Rosabeth Moss Kanter,[9] for example, found that women in business corporations played
special roles not unlike those played by Fairtown's Town
Committee women.   There were few ranking women in the
corporation she studied, and she attributed their seemingly
sex-linked roles and behaviors to their token status.   In
this study the women, though a minority, were not tokens.
Numbers seemed to have little to do with the situation.   The
proportion of women on the two Town Committees differed--
32 percent of the Republicans and 41 percent of the Demo-
crats--yet the roles played on both were linked to gender.
Nor did ideology seem to matter much.   Four of the Democratic women were outspoken feminists; none of the Republicans was.   Yet women played the same unofficial roles
on both parties; indeed, the Democratic Majority Whip was
a staunch feminist.

        In her study of state legislatures Irene Diamond[10]
found that the women there, like the women in Fairtown,
were extraordinarily conscientious, and she asks:

> Is that conscientiousness ... a response to the ex-
> pectation that women are incompetent unless they
> prove otherwise?   Is it their way of adapting to
> their "marginal man" status in the legislature?
> Or is it an outgrowth of sex-role training, a man-
> ifestation of the "tidy housewife" syndrome?   ...
> (or could it be) that these women actually have
> fewer outside conflicts in the allocation of their
> time than male breadwinners?

She does not answer, noting that "the question needs further
exploration."

        I would like to suggest that the overriding reason
men and women take on the roles they do is that these are
the roles they play in our culture wherever men and women
come together in any sort of social organization, the proto-
typical one being the family.   With only minor transforma-
tions the roles the Fairtown men and women were playing

on their Town Committees were the same ones men and
women play in households.   Men are thought to be the "heads"
of their families; and men were the chairpersons of the
Town Committees.   Men have specific and narrow functions
in the family--primarily to provide its income and sometimes to act as its public spokesperson.   So, too, on the
Town Committees they did only what was specifically required
of them.   Women, on the other hand, handle the day-to-day
maintenance of the household, performing a plethora of tasks,
some precisely defined, such as preparing food, but many
amorphous, such as bonding the nuclear family to others
through social contacts.   Similarly, on the Town Committees
all the regular, official maintenance-type functions and also
all tasks that could not be specifically defined fell to women.
Another role women played in both the family and on the
Town Committees was that of standby.   They were there to
step in whenever a man failed to accomplish his appointed
task.

        Women, then, take care of the maintenance of insti-
tutions and fill in the gaps.   They are also the ones to
spot gaps, bringing to the attention of men situations that
call for a decision and monitoring the early stages in decision making--gathering the necessary information and gar-
nering support.   But when it is time to settle an issue, to
make a final decision, men come to the fore.   The analogy
between the family and the political party is so close that
even when it comes to the selection of persons to fill official
positions on the Town Committees and in town government,
patterns characteristic of the family are followed--i.e., men
aggressively seek positions, but women wait to be wooed.

        The tendency among women to work in seclusion
(while men seek to capture center stage) also has antece-
dents in the family.   The women in this study, as in Kanter's and Diamond's, were of the middle class.   It is a
class that has, over the past half-century, suffered some
ambivalence toward work--especially the work that women
do.

        The Protestant ethic places a high value on work,
but, as Thorstein Veblen noted: to be leisured is a sign
of success while manual work is declassé. [11] Before World
War II it was a point of honor with the middle class that
the men did not do menial labor and the women did not labor at all.   Housework was done by paid help.   After the
War household help rose in cost beyond the reach of most

families, so that women who are now past forty (an age
most common among the women on the Town Committees
and in state legislatures) had to take on the menial work
their mothers had spurned. Their situation changed, but
their values did not. So, with the help of tips from wom-
en's magazines, they learned to do their housework in se-
cret. The mark of a well-run household was freshly vac-
uumed carpets, gourmet meals, shiny-faced children, and a
neatly dressed wife-mother who was never seen cooking,
cleaning, or washing, not even by her husband.

When there is political work to do, the same women
who learned to work this magic at home take pains to re-
peat it in the political arena. They are task-oriented, measuring their political performance by completed projects.
The men, on the other hand, garner their self-esteem not
from tasks accomplished but from being included in decision
making. For them, to be seen in a place where decisions
are being made is more important than accomplishing any
task. Carrying this orientation over to the Town Committees, the men did little alone. The significant part of their
political involvement was to appear to be running things, to
appear to be part of the process, to be seen.

These differences have implications for the political
careers of men and women. When work needs to be done,
the women who in the past have so reliably performed tasks
for their party are called upon again. But when ranking
positions are to be filled, it is the men--ever conspicuous
and desirous of titles--who get the nod.

Notes

1Maurice Duverger, The Study of Politics (New York:
Thomas Y. Crowell, 1972), pp. 47-50; V.O. Key, Politics,
Parties, and Pressure Groups (New York: Thomas Y. Crowell, 1978), pp. 589-590; Paul Lazarsfeld, Bernard Berel-
son, and Hazel Gaudet, The People's Choice (New York:
Columbia University Press, 1944); and Seymore Martin Lip-
set, Political Man (Garden City, N.Y.: Doubleday, 1960),
pp. 187-217.
2Hope Chamberlin, A Minority of Members: Women
in the U.S. Congress (New York: Praeger, 1973); Jeane
Kirkpatrick, Political Woman (New York: Basic Books,
1974); Susan Tolchin and Martin Tolchin, Clout: Womanpower and Politics (New York: Capricorn Books, 1976);

Irene Diamond, Sex Roles in the State House (New Haven: Yale University Press, 1977); and Marianne Githens and Jewel L. Prestage, A Portrait of Marginality: The Political Behavior of the American Woman (New York: David McKay, 1977).

3Gabriel A. Almond and Sidney Verba, The Civic Culture: Political Attitudes and Democracy in Five Nations (Boston: Little, Brown, 1963), pp. 224-265; and William Kornhauser, The Politics of Mass Society (Glencoe, Ill.: Free Press, 1959).

4All names of persons and places are fictitious.

5Diamond, Sex Roles in the State House.

6Two of the men and one of the women who did not keep a log resigned from their Town Committees before the study was completed. Two men and one woman refused to keep a log.

7Three of the women who played unofficial roles also held a titular position. However, the unofficial role they played was not a part of their official role. Thus, the Republican "Whip" was her party's secretary, while it was the Vice-Chairperson of the Democratic Party who played that role. The Communicator-in-Chief of the Republican Party was also the Vice-Chairperson, but the Communicator-in-Chief for the Democrats had no official role. No man holding an official position assumed an unofficial one as well.

8Daniel Elazar, American Federalism, 2nd ed. (New York: Thomas Y. Crowell, 1972), pp. 96-98.

9Rosabeth Moss Kanter, Men and Women of the Corporation (New York: Basic Books, 1977).

10Diamond, Sex Roles in the State House.

11Thorstein Veblen, The Theory of the Leisure Class (New York: Mentor Books, 1953).

POLITICAL CULTURE AND SELECTION OF WOMEN JUDGES IN TRIAL COURTS

Beverly Blair Cook

The political culture of a community defines the context within which women aspire to positions in public office, including the judiciary. Variations in cultural features produce different political structures and opportunities for women, which in turn relate to the number and proportion of women on the bench. This study examines the gender composition of the general jurisdiction courts in the fifty-eight largest cities (over 250,000 population). A substantial proportion of the variation in female representation on these courts can be explained by political culture and intervening political variables.

The number of women on the state general-jurisdiction courts in 1977 ranged from none in twenty states[1] to twenty in California. Ten states had a single woman judge; fourteen had two to five, and six had more than five women judges. The number of women on the trial benches of the major metropolitan areas in 1977 varied from none in twenty-six cities to six in Washington, D. C., and Miami; seven in Chicago and Philadelphia; ten in New York City; and fourteen in Los Angeles. In thirteen cities, one woman judge sits among male colleagues. The other thirteen cities have from two to five women judges.

Figure 1 displays the model employed to understand
the pattern of location of women judges in the cities studied.
The basic concept in this model is culture; the linkage between general culture and the selection of women judges is
indirect.   Social culture, political culture, and legal culture
each affects the pattern of location of women in judicial office.   Social culture affects attitudes, roles, and resources
of women, and legal culture affects attitudes, practices, and
experiences that constrain the opportunities for women to
become legal professionals and to hold law jobs.   The social-
and legal-culture portions of the model are ignored in this
paper in order to focus on the political culture, as it affects
the female lawyer's chance for selection to public judicial
office.   A discussion of the concept of culture in general,
political culture and female roles, and political subcultures
in the American context, provide the background for an empirical test of the impact of political culture on female opportunity.   The elements of the political culture sector that
will be identified in the empirical test are political structure, political roles, and political outputs.

The Concept of Culture

The culture of a community, national or local, is
the nonbiological inheritance or social legacy from past gen-
erations. [2]   The psychological dimension of culture is the
internalization by living members of the society of these
standards for action.   Culture is conceptualized as a pattern of deeply rooted and interrelated beliefs, values, and
styles of action.

The first component of culture--beliefs--includes
simplistic notions about the nature and existence of life on
earth, of supernatural beings, and of the natural environment, and also about the source of such knowledge.   Fundamental beliefs are limited to matters significant enough
to affect individual and community life. [3]   The definition of
the status of women is part of the system of beliefs about
sexual differences, which is a major element of every culture. [4]   A belief significant to women is that the ascribed
characteristic of sex is appropriate for assigning social
rights and obligations.   The American culture views the female as dependent and in need of protection. [5]   The epis-
temological belief that this truth was established by a "di-
vine order" or by "the nature of things" allows for change
only by the revision of theology or science.

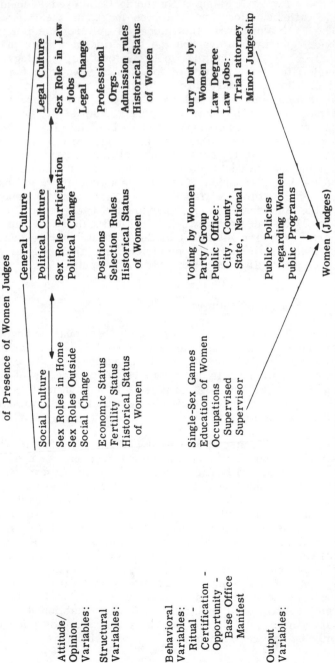

Figure 1

Cultural Model for Explanation
of Presence of Women Judges

The second component of culture--values--includes the ideals and historically associated institutions: for example, free thought and the institution of Science; order and the institution of Law; free choice and Contract; power and War; worship and Religion. The combination of such values with beliefs can have a restrictive impact upon persons classified by ascribed characteristics. The belief that women are weak, emotional, and illogical in a society that values reason and self-control would justify limitations on the roles and rewards of women. Even a quality valued by the society and attributed to a group, such as beauty or sensitivity, might be considered disqualifying for particular responsibilities by the belief system.

The place of women in American society, set by these cultural beliefs and values, has been accurately described by Bardwick and Douvan:[6]

> In spite of an egalitarian ideal in which the role
> and contributions of the sexes are declared to be
> equal and complementary, both men and women
> esteem masculine qualities and achievements....
> When male criteria are the norms against which
> female performance, qualities, or goals are meas-
> ured, then women are not equal. It is not only
> that the culture values masculine productivity more
> than feminine productivity. The essence of the
> derogation lies in the evolution of the masculine
> as the yardstick against which everything is meas-
> ured. Since the sexes are different, women are
> defined as not-men and that means not good, in-
> ferior. It is important to remember that women
> in this culture, as members of the culture, have
> internalized these self-destructive values.

The third component of culture is the style of action or accepted orientation to social problems.[7] These styles or orientations regulate or inform: the definition of public issues as broad or narrow (diffuse/specific); the application of general rules or individualized remedies (universal/particular); categorization of individuals by status or performance (ascribed/achieved); and consideration of personal or public interests (affective/neutral).

The style of the culture has meaning to women or other subgroups in combination with particular beliefs and values. During a period of transition away from the belief

in female inferiority, a particularistic or affective orientation by male elites might be more rewarding than application
of universal and neutral rules rooted in the traditional society. Even ascriptive classification, as used in affirmative-
action programs, and diffuse definitions of a problem, as
in the rule of "pattern and practice of discrimination," are
styles with short-term utility.

Political Culture

        Political culture consists of a subset of the beliefs,
values, and styles of the general culture, which gives shape
to political structures and behavior. Verba defines the political culture as "the system of empirical beliefs, expressive symbols, and values which defines the situation in which
political action takes place."[8] Rosenbaum defines political
culture as the collective orientation toward government structure, government authority, and individual roles in the polity. The political culture is rooted in the same historical
experience as the general culture, although the dimensions
may be somewhat differentiated.[9]

        The core beliefs describe what social concerns are
in the public realm and what classes of persons are participants in politics. Values indicate the proper rule of
distribution of goods through the political process and provide measures for the legitimacy of political actors and their
policy outputs.[10] The style of politics may be patronage
(affective) or reform (neutral); open and formal (universa-
listic) or closed and bargained (particularistic).

        Elites often fashion the political system in their own
image and "may epitomize with particular clarity the dominant political orientations of the population as a whole."[11]
Instead of examining the elite "carriers of the culture," Almond and Verba try to understand political culture through
the attitudes of the ordinary members of political communities. Their work is an exploration of mass attitudes toward political phenomena, which would generally reflect the
more basic beliefs, styles, and values. They define the
"civic culture" in terms of the efficacy, competency, and
political activity of the citizens, and report that American
women are sufficiently competent, active, and involved in
politics to classify the United States as a civic culture.[12]

Female Role in the Political Culture

The cultural stereotyping of woman as dependent and
man as protector carries over to the rationalization of role
differentiation in political life. Greenstein[13] notes the limitations placed by the culture upon the participation of the
majority of adult women. According to Lane:[14]

> A major feature of our culture's typing of the two
> sexes is the assignment of the ascendant, power-
> possessing role to the man and the dependent, re-
> ceptive role to the woman. ... But since the senti-
> ment is still present in a persistently strong de-
> gree, it is certain to affect the cultural perspec-
> tives in any area closely associated with gaining
> and wielding power. Politics is precisely such
> an area of power, and a woman enters politics
> only at the risk of tarnishing, to some extent, her
> femininity. Although voting and talking politics
> are only at the threshold of this power-saturated
> area of life, the woman who seems too active in
> these areas seems, to some people, to have moved
> from the properly dependent role of her sex and to
> seek the masterful and dominant role of men.

The belief that politics is a male arena of action was
too deep-seated to disappear when the Nineteenth Amendment
passed in 1920. In 1924 Merriam and Gosnell[15] discovered
that women still thought "voting is a man's business," and
in 1948 the Erie County Study reported responses that "voting is for the man."[16] Even though voting is a ritual act,
the right to vote identifies members of the political community. For women the suffrage symbolized their equal share
of public responsibility. The increasing participation by
women in this national ritual after 1960 shows that the old
belief in the assignment of males to political work has erod-
ed in the face of contradictory law and behavior.[17]

Aside from the ritual of voting, American women can
be described as "subjects," as the term is employed by Almond and Verba. The subject obeys the law but is not an
active participant in its shaping.[18] Although female members of the American political community are patriotic--
i.e., allegiant[19]--they lack representation among the elite,
which would allow identification of themselves with the regime.
As the authors of The Civic Culture point out: "If he has

more education, higher status, or is male, he is clearly
more likely to consider himself competent. "[20] Women in
their study discussed politics less than men, had less political information, and felt more apathetic about political
matters. [21]

Nevertheless, the authors report that American wom-
en express a responsibility to participate in local politics,
since 50 percent (compared to 52 percent of the men) "say
the Ordinary Man Should Be Active in His Local Community. "
The exact question did not have as obvious a bias as the cap-
tion on the table--i.e., "We know that the ordinary person
has many problems that take his time. In view of this, what
part do you think the ordinary person ought to play in the
local affairs of his town or district?"[22] The similarity of
percentage responses by sex may not reveal that women
view themselves as participant but that women understand
the appropriate male role. As socializers of male children
they can report accurately on role expectations for both
sexes. The notion that female respondents would reply as
to the male political role is supported by the male-oriented
bias of the entire survey. [23]

In their comparative study of participation Almond
and Verba try to fit the less-politically-involved American
women into their scheme by positing complementary political
roles assigned by sex within the family. [24] But if the woman's role is political socializer within the family, she cannot be accurately described as participant in the larger political system. The device of conceptualizing the family
rather than the individual as the political actor fits with the
ancient legal rule of the "oneness" of marital partners and
the encapsulation of women in a family unit headed by a
male who carries out the political and legal obligations. The
modern style of marriage and divorce makes such a conceptualization unrealistic.

It is fair to conclude that the dominant studies of
political participation simply underreport the stringent cultural limitations upon women in our society. From one perspective, this failure to perceive cultural limitations is un-
derstandable, since the patterns of culture are accepted at
an unconscious level by those who participate in the polity. [25]
Daniel Elazar suggests that, the limits and directions of political behavior are "more effective because of their antiquity
and subtlety whereby those limited are unaware of the limitations placed upon them. "[26] The cultural norms cover what

demands, what decision-making persons and processes, and
what policy outputs are suitable. The individual living within the culture accepts at a subconscious level the limitations
on what it is possible to ask for or expect from a particular
institution. If the cultural patterns reveal few opportunities
for women to become political authorities or to pursue wom-
en's interests through political processes, then female members of the society are unlikely to think of such a possibility
or to consider the idea feasible.

For women whose "consciousness is raised" to the
obvious, there is dismay and anger at their own failure to
perceive their shackles and at their cooperation in their own
victimization. The subtlety even extends to individuals' capacity to remove some scales from their eyes while leaving
others in place. All of this applies to understanding wom-
en who attain judicial office.

Women who move into the man's world of the law
and the bench may be willing to accept restrictions not
placed upon men in the same position. For some women
this is an automatic acceptance of the rules of the game,
which limit the perquisites when a woman takes over a male
role. To other women it is a calculated choice of gradual
over radical change. Since the stability of the political organizations depends upon their functioning in harmony with
the political culture, incremental change has the practical
virtue of maintaining the effectiveness of the institution wom-
en have just joined. [27]

The woman who attains the bench against the cultural
odds still performs in a milieu that defines her as unsuited.
To the extent that her physical image emphasizes her membership in the wrong gender class, adjustment is more difficult. Taking a high-status role defined as belonging to the
male sex puts the woman in a precarious and vulnerable situation, open to criticism and derision regardless of her concrete behavior. [28] Mead states that "the whole symbolic system ... facilitates every step taken by the expected sex, ob-
structs every step taken by the unexpected sex."[29] The more
deeply rooted and ancient the one-sex cultural pattern, the
more destructive and difficult the adjustment to two sexes
sharing the same role.

In addition to defining "who should serve," the political culture also provides the standards for measuring the
performance of political authorities. Acceptance of a woman

judge depends upon her adherence to the inherited norms. Merit and ability do not exist apart from particular standards and are not measured by universal, extracultural standards. There is little room even for the brilliant woman to effect major changes in procedures and policies. Her career security depends upon her general acceptance of the old norms; her contributions are limited to what she can do while maintaining her legitimacy as a public figure representative of the community's culture. Those identified as deviants in any other way except gender are vulnerable to criticism and removal from power. Challenges to the culture are somewhat easier (although less likely) from those who fit the stereotype of ascriptions. Women judges probably cannot make major changes in policy outputs while their gender identifies them as authorities on probation.

Political Subcultures

The cultural stereotyping of women as dependent on male protectors operates to limit female opportunity in general. However, some variation in the power of this stereotype might be presumed to exist across political subcultures. Within the national political culture there are subcultures associated with somewhat different values regarding the public interest, and different styles of decision making. Elazar[30] has identified three important subcultures in the United States associated with streams of ethnic-religious migrations. In the traditional subculture the range of governmental interests is limited to the preservation of the existing social order and participation is restricted to the elite from established families. In the individualist subculture government extends its agenda to economic and social problems in response to demands, and the motivation of political participation is private, not public, interest. In the moralist subculture government takes responsibility for the good society, concerning itself with a broad range of issues and expecting participation of citizens as a public duty.

Elazar[31] designates the geographical locations of these subcultures in mainland United States by drawing subjective judgments from a variety of data. Sharkansky[32] tested Elazar's culture categories in relation to several dimensions of contemporary political activity that could be predicted to relate to the theory. He discovered that the "closest and most consistent relationships are with variables pertaining to participation." The independent variable of culture was not an artifact of region, income level, or urbanism of the state.[33]

Sharkansky concluded that the Elazar concept would be useful for political analyses if appropriate indicators were empirically developed.

      Monroe[34] generated scores for the three subcultures
in each Illinois county by factor analyses of native, ethnic,
and religious migration statistics and party voting patterns.
He concludes that "it is possible to systematically and quan-
titatively measure the historical sources of cultural variation
within the American states, that the Elazar schema does
seem to be verified as a general pattern, and that the meas-
urement of cultural streams can be useful in explaining current patterns of political life."[35]

      Johnson[36] creates indicators for the subculture more
simply by the average population percentage of the major religious denominations in each state in four census years
(1906, 1916, 1926, and 1936). He used discriminant analysis to compare Elazar's subjective categorization of states
to his own quantitative categorization.[37] Seven states that
Elazar classified as moralistic were individualist by Johnson's measure; two individualist states were moralist; and
four traditional states were individualist.[38] Johnson finds
that popular participation is highest in the moralist states
and lowest in the traditional states; and party strength and
salience greatest in the individualist states.[39]

Female Role in Political Subcultures

      The opportunity for women to gain public office will
be shaped differently by the subcultures. Holding public office has less of the quality of ritual than voting. The assignment of public office to males has persisted because the
rewards are greater than voting. However, women would
be more likely to be allowed to share in those rewards in
a subculture that valued participation. The moralist culture
has several characteristics taht suggest that the obligation
to participate would apply to both sexes. First, it is a
rationalist culture, which could not easily blind itself to the
illogic of excluding over half the voters from an opportunity
for higher public service. Second, it recognizes as a matter of public concern the kinds of social problems--children,
poverty, exploitation--with which women have historical experience in the private institutions, such as settlement houses.
Third, it attaches importance to government activity at local
levels, thus providing a political arena for part-time, ama-
teur politicians.

Participation is most restricted for both sexes in the traditional subculture and is monopolized by party activists in the individualist culture. In response to national demands for the inclusion of women in public office, state political systems in each subculture would respond in ways which required the least adjustment of their cultural patterns. Different types of women would be predicted to win judgeships through different processes in each subculture.

The traditional culture could adjust to the intrusion of women at the lowest cost by accepting the female members of the established elite. The crack in the traditional culture for the unusual woman is its emphasis upon a historical elite inheriting the right to govern through family and social ties. Where a woman is the only or the brightest product of a political and legal family, then the sex barrier may fall in order to preserve the narrow power base. Such women would not be expected to bring to court feminist views that would change the agendas or the substance of public policy. They would be conservative and would differ from their peers only as to gender. Most women selected from the proper background would accept the terms of selection at an unconscious level. The insightful woman who understands the unwritten contract would be unlikely to stake her position against the risk of trying to change the cultural attitude toward nonelite women.

Participation in politics in the individualist culture provides personal rewards; so that the ambitious, upwardly mobile woman would not be out of place. She would pay her dues for the judicial office by making the same contribution to party work as her male colleagues. Her ability to pursue a woman's agenda would depend upon the strength of the organized woman's movement in the state and local political system. Without feminist-group support of her candidacy, the female officeholder would have no incentive to work for feminist policy goals on the basis of principle. Female candidates for office could include all classes--poor and ethnic minorities as well as middle-class and elite members who had earned their legal and political credentials. Like the male judges, the women would respond to constituent demands; to the extent that the constituencies included poor and ethnic groups, they would identify and respond with policy initiatives more than women in the other subcultures.

In the moralist subculture the acceptance of women in public office can be demanded on the basis of the shared value

of civic participation. Women who agree with the principles
of the "commonwealth" can be admitted to positions of power
more safely than men who are private-regarding. The style
of the subculture suits the typical modes of participation of
middle-class women in consensual organizations that pursue
the public interest. Women with personal ambition would
have to cloak it behind the image of the selfless public ser-
vant.

The historical development of the women's movement
during the nineteenth century prepared women to meet the
standards of the moralist culture. The leaders who eventually won the suffrage victory promised that women would
use the vote to improve society, to protect the family, to
inculcate the young and alien to cultural norms, and to gain
world peace. They asked for the untraditional tool of the
vote to achieve traditional goals; and the untraditional role
of public officeholder is suited to similar traditional goal
seeking in the moralist culture. The moralist culture is
also concerned with reform of structure and people; and the
development of the profession of social work by women re-
sulted in the definition of reform "as a women's field."[40]
Although Lane saw the female custody of moral values as a
consolation prize for exclusion from power,[41] the female
image and experience fit a political career in the moralist
culture. The reform style, however, may not prepare the
incumbents to deal effectively with women's issues.

The distribution of the women judges among the states
fits the prediction based on political culture. There are
twice as many women judges on the appellate level in the
moralist as the individualist or traditionalist states; and
more than twice as many on the minor-court level. However, differences appear less important on the general-jurisdiction trial courts, with fifty-nine women judges in the
moralist states, forty-four in the individualist states, and
thirty-one in the traditional states (see Table 1). The proportion of women on the benches is also higher in the moralist culture. The barriers raised by the party organization
in the individualist culture and by the sex-role stereotyping
in the traditional culture have a similar impact upon the opportunity for women to become public authorities.

Empirical Test of the Culture Model

A more refined measure for political culture is

achieved by Sharkansky's[42] scoring of the Elazar data,
which ranges from one for a moralist culture to nine for
a traditional culture.   In applying that measure to cities in
the study, we find that none has a predominantly traditional
culture.   The city scores range from one to six, or moralist to individualist combined with minor traditionalist aspects.   There is a direct simple correlation in the expected
direction between culture and the number of women judges
in the cities (-. 275), showing the larger number of women
judges in moralist places.

Such a correlation does not explain much of the variation among the cities.   A more elaborate model may show
that culture works indirectly through other social and political phenomena to affect opportunities for women in government.   Two structural and two behavioral variables are introduced as intervening variables between culture and number of women judges.   The structural characteristics of the
courts are the size or number of trial judges and the model
of selection.   The behavioral variables are the number of
city women who attended the party nominating conventions
in 1976 and the index of services available to women in the
cities.   A path analysis is an appropriate method for finding
out if the culture works through the contemporary processes
and conditions rather than affecting the dependent variable
directly.   Table 2 depicts the results of this analysis.

The structural variables have the expected relationship to the culture.   In the moralist culture the benches
are typical of reform systems, with more judges and selection by appointment rather than election.   One would expect that women would have less access to any set of offices
limited in number; but that female intrusion would be possible where more "goods" or offices were available for all.
There is a strong correlation between size of bench and number of women judges.   The path from moral culture to bench
size is as predicted (-. 113); and the path from bench size
to number of women judges (+. 410).   Since the benches are
larger in the reorganized court systems of the moralist culture, the factors of culture and availability of positions reinforce each other.

The structure of selection is operationalized by the
number of persons participating in the choice.   Partisan
election involves the largest constituency and is scored one.
Gubernatorial appointment without advice is scored nine.[43]
The moralist culture emphasizes qualifications over demo-

Table 1

Women Judges by Political Culture and Court Level

Culture	#States	Appellate #Judges	Women	%	General Jurisdiction #Judges	Women	%	Minor* #Judges	Women	%
Moral	20	286	14	4.9	1845	59	3.2	1866	121	6.5
Individual	14	251	7	2.8	1754	44	2.5	1194	52	4.4
Traditional	16	276	7	2.5	1547	31	2.0	890	40	4.5

*Limited jurisdiction courts where judge is required to be an attorney.

Moralist: Those ten states categorized as M by both Elazar and Johnson; plus nine states categorized as M by one only; and Alaska.

Individualist: Those thirteen states categorized as I by both Elazar and Johnson; and Hawaii.

Traditionalist: Those twelve states categorized as T by both Elazar and Johnson, and four categorized as T. by Elazar only.

Table 2

Culture, Structure, and Politics Affecting Number of Women Judges

Complete Path Model Matrix for Women Judges in 58 Cities

	Elazar	Size of Bench	Mode of Selection	Number of Delegates	Services for Women	Number of Women Judges
	1	2	3	4	5	6
1	-					
2	-.113					
3	-.318	.000				
4	-.216	.685	.000			
5	.000	.000	.200	.406		
6	.000	.410	.000	.434	.131	

% of Variation Explained by Path Coefficients: 37.4
% of Variation Explained by Correlation: 33.3
% of Variation Explained by Residuals: 29.2

R = .841

R^2 = .708

cratic accountability, preferring the reform modes of appointment, particularly with recommendations from professional
sources. The correlation between moralist culture and the
reform mode of selection is strong (-.318). However, the
selection structure does not explain the number of women
judges. The voters or the governor are equally likely or
unlikely to choose women for the bench. Women lawyers
with ambition for the bench evidently have to learn to work
within whatever selection structure exists in their community.

        The political-behavior concept is operationalized by
the number of women participating in party politics by attending the 1976 national conventions as delegates. The
figures for each convention indicated that each party selected
more women delegates from cities where the party was
weak. Therefore, the indicator is the number of Democratic women delegates where the dominant party is Democratic; and of Republican women where the dominant party
is Republican. Party dominance in the city was measured
by the number of city representatives in the state legislature of each party. The moralist culture had a larger number of female delegates; and where women were active in
party politics more women were on the bench.

        The concept of public policy is operationalized by the
number of services provided for women in the community.
The indicator ranges from zero to four, depending upon how
many of the following services are available in each city:
a rape hotline or support facility, an abortion clinic, a feminist health center, and a Commission on the Status of Wom-
en.[44] There are more services where there are more wom-
en active in party politics. The feminist policy has much
less effect upon the presence of women judges than the elements of political competition and participation. The significance of policy output is in the feedback effect upon wom-
en's participation in ritual and organized politics rather than
as candidates for office.

        The coefficient of determination that describes the
combined explanatory power of the five variables is 71 percent. The political-culture model fails to explain only 27
percent of the variation in number of women judges among
the cities. Culture does not operate directly in affecting
the number of women judges, but works indirectly through
the four intervening structural and behavioral variables,
contributing 20 percent of the total 71 percent explanation.

The most important variables are clearly one structural
variable, the size of the bench, and one behavioral variable,
the political activity of local women.   The local services
for women correlate directly less strongly.

The model can be used to estimate the number of
women judges in each city.   The model has greater utility
for some cities than others.   Six cities that currently have
no women judges fit the model and are unlikely to accept
women on the bench in the near future: El Paso, Birming-
ham, Baton Rouge, Norfolk, Tampa, and Wichita.   Other
cities have more women on the bench than expected, and
other explanations are needed to understand women's greater
opportunities for law jobs in these cities: Los Angeles,
Miami, and Jacksonville.   Other cities had fewer women
on the bench than estimated, and other explanations are
needed to explain why their access to the bench is blocked.
Houston had three less; San Francisco, Detroit, Atlanta,
and Minneapolis, two less; and Dallas, Milwaukee, Columbus, Louisville, and Akron, one less than expected.   Since
there are favorable cultural conditions in those ten cities,
some organized efforts for women candidates might well
pay off.   In fact, since 1977, the date of the data on which
this study was based, two women (one more than estimated)
have been appointed in Milwaukee.

Culture Model and Percentage of Women Judges

The cultural variables predict the absolute number of
women better than the proportion of women judges found in
each by city.   The coefficient of determination for the percentage on the city bench is 31 percent, considerably less
than 71 percent.   The culture has a direct as well as an
indirect effect upon the percentage of women city judges.
Otherwise, the pattern of relationships is similar for member and percentage of women judges per bench.

The percentage of women on a court shows how much
of this valuable political resource male politicians are willing to share.   Acceptance of a token woman on a court is
more significant in Indianapolis, where the single woman constitutes 8.3 percent of the bench, than in New Orleans,
where she takes 4.2 percent of the share of seats.   Women
judges have 10 percent or more of the general jurisdiction
positions in only ten cities: Washington, D.C., Jacksonville,
Denver, Seattle, Portland, Newark, Miami, Tulsa, Tucson,

and Jersey City. Even more significant is the fact that the culture model indicates underrepresentation only in Boston, Kansas City, Minneapolis, Omaha, Louisville, and St. Paul.

The model in this study includes the deep-seated and slowly changing culture with less permanent structural and behavioral features of society to understand the number of women in judgeships. The finding is that culture affects women's opportunities for political office indirectly, working through its effect upon contemporary organization and behavior. Even when community mores and the immediate situation are favorable, there must be women prepared to take advantage of those conditions. The explanation missing from this model may be found in the size of the pool of female candidates ready for the judicial position; and that is the next logical direction for research on this topic.

Notes

[1]Alabama, Alaska, Delaware, Idaho, Kentucky, Maine, Missouri, Montana, Nebraska, Nevada, New Hampshire, New Mexico, North Carolina, North Dakota, South Carolina, Tennessee, Utah, Vermont, Virginia, and Wyoming.

[2]Talcott Parsons, Essays on Social Theory (New York: Free Press, 1949), p. 8; and Clyde Kluckhorn, Mirror for Man (New York: McGraw-Hill, 1949), p. 17.

[3]This conceptualization differs from Rikeach in not including a piece of information--such as the landing of Columbus in 1492--as a belief. Ideas about the shape of the earth and the role of women in exploration would constitute beliefs.

[4]Jessie Barnard, "The Status of Women in Modern Patterns of Culture," in Cynthia F. Epstein and William J. Goode, eds., The Other Half (Englewood Cliffs, N.J.: Prentice-Hall, 1971), p. 11.

[5]Margaret Mead, Male and Female: A Study of the Sexes in a Changing World (New York: Morrow, 1949), p. 290.

[6]Judith M. Bardwick and Elizabeth Douvan, "Ambivalence: The Socialization of Women," in Vivian Gornick and Barbara K. Moran, eds., Women in Sexist Society (New York: Basic Books, 1971).

[7]Talcott Parsons and Edward A. Shils, Toward a General Theory of Action (Cambridge: Harvard University Press, 1951).

[8]Lucian W. Pye and Sidney Verba, eds., Political

59   Selection of Women Judges

Culture and Political Development (Princeton: Princeton
University Press, 1965).
        9Daniel Elazar, Cities of the Prairie: The Metro-
politan Frontier and American Politics (New York: Basic
Books, 1970), p. 256.
        10Samuel C. Patterson, American Legislative Be-
havior (Princeton: Van Nostrand, 1968), p. 277.
        11Rosenbaum, p. 26.
        12Gabriel A. Almond and Sidney Verba, The Civic
Culture: Political Attitudes and Democracy in Five Nations
(Princeton: Princeton University Press, 1963).
        13Fred W. Greenstein, "Sex-Related Political Differ-
ences in Childhood," Journal of Politics 23 (1961):   353-371.
        14Robert E. Lane, Political Life (New York: Free
Press, 1959), p. 213.
        15Charles E. Mirriam and Harold F. Gosnell, Non-
Voting (Chicago: University of Chicago Press, 1924), p. 47.
        16Paul F. Lazarsfeld, Bernard B. Berelson, and
Hazel Guadet, The People's Choice (New York: Columbia
University Press, 1948), p. 49.
        17The differences in percentage of males and females
voting for President declined from 1948 to 1972:   1948--13
percent; 1952--10 percent; 1956--11 percent; 1960--11 per-
cent; 1964--3 percent; 1968--3 percent; 1972--6 percent.
Data taken from Jane Jaquette, ed., Women in Politics
(New York: John Wiley, 1974), Table 1.2, p. 8.
        18Almond and Verba, The Civic Culture, pp. 19, 162.
        19Ibid., pp. 389-396.
        20Ibid., pp. 212-220.
        21Ibid.
        22Ibid., p. 169, fn. 11.
        23Ibid., Appendix 3, pp. 528-529.
        24Ibid., p. 398.
        25Elazar, Cities of the Prairie, p. 256.
        26Ibid., p. 257.
        27Patterson, American Legislative Behavior, p. 277.
        28Mead, Male and Female, p. 351.
        29Ibid., p. 354.
        30Daniel Elazar, American Federalism: A View from
the States (New York: Thomas Y. Crowell, 1966).
        31Ibid., pp. 14-15.
        32Ira Sharkansky, Regionalism in American Politics
(Indianapolis: Bobbs-Merrill, 1969), p. 83.
        33Ibid., Table 5, p. 81, and Table 6, p. 82.   The
moralist culture was also strongly associated with high levels of support for education and welfare.   This is noted in
Elazar, American Federalism.

34Alan D. Monroe, "Operationalizing Political Culture: The Illinois Case," Publius 6 (Winter 1977): 107-120.
35Ibid., p. 116.
36Charles A. Johnson, "Political Culture in the American States: Elazar's Formulation Examined," American
Journal of Political Science 20 (August 1976): 491-507.
37Ibid., Table 2, pp. 496-497.
38The twelve traditional states that fit that category
for both Elazar and Johnson are: Alabama, Arkansas, Florida, Georgia, Kentucky, Mississippi, North Carolina, Okla-
homa, South Carolina, Tennessee, Texas, and Virginia. The
inclusion of Florida is questionable, since large groups with
economic and social resources have arrived from nontradi-
tional cultures. While a culture may incorporate, ignore,
or sanction migratory groups without resources, such as
blacks moving North, a culture may be effected more rapid-
ly by the settlement of ethnic groups with resources. The
individualist culture that Elazar shows in the Miami area
and moving North would not be revealed by Johnson's historical census measures.
39Johnson, "Political Culture in American States,"
pp. 503-504, Table 4.
40Mead, Male and Female, p. 292.
41Lane, Political Life, p. 212.
42Sharkansky, Regionalism in American Politics.
43Scale for Selection Structure: Partisan election =
1; Nonpartisan election = 2; Legislative selection = 3; Judicial convention = 4; Federal System = 5; Missouri plan
= 6; statutory advisory commission = 7; Ad Hoc advisory
commission = 8; Governor alone = 9.
44Data for this index were collected by Cathie An-
derson in an independent study project. T-Ratio for each
item was < .001; Cronbach's alpha = .381.

THE EFFECTS OF SEX ON RECRUITMENT: CONNECTICUT LOCAL OFFICES

Susan Gluck Mezey

Political recruitment is an indispensable function of a political system.[1] Since women have not been very active in the ranks of society's political elite until recently, they have been virtually ignored in the literature on recruitment of elites into political roles.[2] Many studies of women in politics stress the difficulties that women encounter when they enter political office; however, there is increasing evidence that while women office-holders may suffer disadvantages vis à vis their male counterparts, most of their problems arise before they enter public office.

Women contemplating political careers are often inhibited by the dual problems of sex-role conditioning, which molds them into subordinate and passive roles, and external constraints, such as responsibility for child care and home-making, which impinge upon their ability to seek outlets beyond traditional ones. Sexual differentiation in the socialization process often discourages women from being interested in the political process. Numerous studies document the fact that women as a group are less interested, less involved, and less active in politics.[3] By concentrating on the women who remain politically inert, political scientists have neglected the women who are recruited into active political roles and have ignored the special circumstances of female political recruitment.

61

This study begins by examining the political opportunity structure and recruitment process for women that has been described in the literature and then focuses on the specific experiences of one group of political women--local representatives in the State of Connecticut.

Limits on Women's Access to Political Roles

There has been a good deal of discussion of the various factors that limit women's opportunities in the political world. Although socialization and sex-role conditioning were once offered as the primary reasons why women were not very active political participants,[4] it is now apparent that other obstacles confront women and contribute to their lesser involvement in political affairs. While the socialization theory has not been completely discarded, it has been supplemented by theories proclaiming the importance of situational and structural restraints upon women.[5] Briefly, socialization theorists tell us that women do not want to become politically active because of internal restraints, while situational and structural theorists tell us that they cannot due to external constraints. Family responsibilities and household duties are typically offered as situational pressure, while the lack of occupational qualifications are cited as structural restrictions. As Welch tells us: "These explanations are neither contradictory nor mutually exclusive. All might be working together, or the situational variables may contribute to and perpetuate the distinct political socialization patterns."[6] Although these theories have been primarily used to explain male-female differences in political participation among the mass public, they can also be used to clarify and explain male-female differences in the recruitment of political elites.[7]

Family Responsibilities

Most women are socialized to become wives and mothers and led to believe that family obligations must precede all others. While this belief prevents many women from seeking political responsibilities in addition to their family responsibilities, it does not stop them all. One effect of this conditioning, however, is that women who enter public life usually do so at more advanced ages than their male colleagues. This age difference has been found at all levels of public office--from local public officials to members

of the United States Congress.[8] Whether women serve as
local representatives, members of the state legislature, or
of the United States House of Representatives, there is typically more delay for them than for men in making the decision to seek public office; such delay means that the majority of women do not begin political careers until their
childbearing and -rearing years are over.

Another problem confronting politically active women
is support from their spouses; there is evidence that women
are more dependent upon support from home than men are.
One study of state legislators found women legislators received
more support and encouragement from their husbands than males
received from their wives. The study concluded that women are
probably less likely to run for legislative office unless their husbands are positive and supportive.[9] Another study of female
state legislators stressed that cooperative husbands are a necessity for married women who want to go into politics.[10]

Whether family obligations and responsibilities that
prevent, or at best, delay women in the pursuit of political
careers should be classified as socialization or situational
factors is a subject of much futile debate; but no single explanation can account for the disparity between male and female political participation. It may be that women are socialized into roles that impose structural obstacles to office
holding.   Putting aside the debate on causality, it is clear
that sex differences in political roles are a microcosm of
sex differences in societal roles.   Jennings and Thomas's
1968 study of male and female delegates to national nominating conventions argued that basic sex-role differentiation
was responsible for inequities between male and female delegates and concluded that "any change in the direction of
feminine equality among political elites will occur only
through a more profound social revolution which alters basic sex roles in that direction.   Only when women come to
the point of sharing equally in other occupations and roles
prized and dominated by males may we expect to see this
equity."[11]

Occupational Criteria

The major structural variable cited to explain wom-
en's limited political participation is restricted access to
careers and occupations that serve as stepping-stones to
political careers.   Several studies on recruitment of political

elites stress that they are chosen from certain strata of
society and must possess certain background characteristics. 12   The requirements usually include occupational, educational, racial, and sexual criteria.   Occupations typically
leading to political careers are law or business; college
graduates in any field are more likely to gain political office, and white males are vastly overrepresented in the
ranks of the political elite.   Social-role differentiation that
puts women in subordinate positions in general societal roles
leads directly to the structural factors limiting their access
to political roles should they desire to pursue them.

Discrimination

        Women's political opportunity structure is also lim-
ited by discrimination. 13   Welch argues that while discrimination only plays an indirect role in participation in routine
political acts, "when we examine a different form of political
activity--such as running for office or directing a campaign
--it is undoubtedly true that discrimination is more direct...."14   Discrimination may work against women at any
stage in the selection process; there is mounting evidence,
however, that it is largely felt during the early stages of
the political-recruitment process. 15

        Many women politicians, having hurdled the obstacles
of their private lives and family obligations, point to the
party bureaucracy and leadership as the real source of discrimination against women in politics.   It is well documented
that party control of political recruitment is a major road-
block for aspiring women. 16   In her book on women members of Congress, Peggy Lamson states: "If blame is to be
attached to any group of men it must not be to those who
pull the voting machine lever inside the polling booth but to
those who pull the strings inside the political parties."17
In sum, women are often deterred from elite political roles
and kept from positions of power because there are men in
party hierarchies who act as gate keepers and allow only
small numbers of them to pass through.

        This view is further reinforced by studies that con-
clude that sex is not a very significant factor in the voting
booth.   The effects of sex are largely felt before women get
their names on the ballot.   In an analysis of local elections
the authors conclude: "Our data suggest that the main problems are associated with becoming candidates rather than

gaining election after female candidates are on the ballot."[18]
The same conclusions were drawn by the authors of a study
on male and female candidates in congressional elections.[19]
When controlling for the effects of party and incumbency in
a number of elections from 1972 to 1974, the authors note
that sex plays only a minimal role, if any, in electoral out-
comes.   Women's major problems occur in the recruitment
and nomination processes; once nominated, their sex does
not appear to be a major detriment to electoral success.
A study of women in the 1976 state legislative elections also placed blame for limitations in the political opportunity
structure on party leaders by stating: "Party leaders recruited relatively few nonincumbent women candidates to run
in districts where chances of electoral success were good.
In approximately half the cases where party leaders actively
sought out and encouraged women to run for office, it appears that they were recruiting candidates to serve as sacrificial lambs."[20]   Similarly, Diamond notes that women's opportunities for political office are greatest in the absence of
competition for legislative seats.[21]

      The pattern of sexual discrimination against women
from male party leaders appears to be pervasive.   However, the party also represents an available avenue of recruitment for politically aspiring women; women have always been major contributors of time and effort to party
activities.   Diamond has documented the importance of party
ties to women who have made it to political office;[22] others
have noted the energies that women have donated to party
activities;[23] and one study found that women have been able
to use party experience to compensate for educational and
occupational disadvantages they suffer vis-à-vis their male
colleagues.[24]

Women in Municipal Office: Connecticut

      Local governments have always offered women the
greatest opportunity to serve as public officials.   It is argued that women find it easier to gain acceptance at the
local level of office and that they seek out these positions
because they are closer to traditional local issues.[25]   Whatever the cause, the percentage of women officeholders is
higher at the municipal than at the state or federal level.
It is ironic, therefore, that even though most women have
been associated with local political office, with one or two
exceptions[26] there has been little specifically written on

their access and recruitment to this office. Most studies
focus on women at the state legislative level, [27] or at the
congressional level [28] or at national nominating conventions. [29]
Since local office differs from other levels of office on several dimensions, including its acceptance of women, this
study examines the political socialization and recruitment of
women in local offices only while paying particular attention
to the role of the political party. Hypotheses will be derived from studies of women at higher levels of public office.

     Connecticut women have somewhat of an advantage
in their pursuit of local office; they constitute roughly 13
percent of local legislators--slightly higher than the national
average of about 10 percent. Perhaps the state's greater
acceptance of women officeholders, seen by the number of
female state legislators (20.3 percent in 1977), accounts for
this higher figure; or maybe Connecticut's particular form
of local government or party structure is also partially responsible. Whatever the reason, just as Connecticut provides a good laboratory for the study of women in state office [30] it also provides a good laboratory for the study of
women at the local level.

Local Governments and Political Parties

     Connecticut is particularly well suited to a study of
local government, since political participation is closely tied
to town meetings and local legislative governing bodies in the
169 towns within the state. Town governments represent an
important part of community life; recently the state has even
increased its efforts to "encourage effective local services
and to strengthen the financial ability of towns to provide
these services." [31] Eight towns still conform to the original
New England town-meeting model, while the remainder have
adapted the model to suit their particular needs. Most municipalities today are governed by legislative bodies; these
range from a three-member Board of Selection to a twenty
to twenty-five seat Town Council or Board of Aldermen.

     The importance of the political party in Connecticut
also cannot be overemphasized; elections to town office revolve around the two major political parties, which are organized hierarchically with a state central committee at the
top. The sixty-nine town committees are the basic units of
organization of the two major parties in the state. The

parties play a vital role in the political recruitment process, since nominees to local office are selected by the party committee in each town. Town party committees also select delegates to conventions at which all nominees for office above the local level are selected. According to the League of Women Voters, "Connecticut parties are remarkable among states in the degree of control that the party leadership is able to exercise over candidates and policy."[32]

The Sample

Fifty female politicians were randomly selected to be interviewed from towns and cities in Connecticut that had women representatives on the local legislative bodies; the selection was based upon a stratified random sample according to the size of the municipality. Personal interviews lasting from one-half hour to two hours were conducted with each respondent. A corresponding sample of fifty male officeholders was also selected. To focus on sex differences, the survey matched the males to the women by town, age, and party affiliation; whenever possible, respondents were also matched by length of time in office. The matching procedure was relaxed when circumstances required, as in small towns with a three-member Board of Selectmen; in every case, however, females and their matched male respondents were members of the same board or council. As illustrated in Table 1, representatives from forty-one town and city councils were included in the survey.

A comparison of the ages and number of years in office as well as the political-party affiliations reveals that the matching attempts were successful. The average age of women respondents was 47.3, of men 45.4; the average number of years in office was three for the women and 3.5 years for the men. Thirty-one women and thirty-four men were Democrats, eighteen women and fifteen men were Republicans, and one woman and one man were members of a locally based Independent Conservative Party.

Recruitment and Social Status

Although government leaders are all inclined to be chosen from the "more prestigious occupations, the better-educated or otherwise privileged members of the community,"[33] most analysts have found disparities between male and female political leaders. These disparities, reflections

Table 1

Number of Women Respondents and Number of

Towns Sampled in Each Size Category

Size of Town	Number Women Sampled[a]	Number Towns Sampled[b]
Under 5,000	5	5
5,001 to 15,000	11	10
15,001 to 25,000	12	12
25,001 to 50,000	6	5
Over 50,000	16	9
Total	50	41

[a]Men were selected from the same towns as the women.

[b]More than one woman representative was selected in the following municipalities: Monroe (2); Manchester (2); Danbury (2); New Haven (3); Waterbury (2); and Stamford (4). The Municipalities were divided into five size categories, and the number of women from each of the five groups was calculated as a percentage of the total number of women in office; this percentage was then computed as a percentage of the total sample size. The female officeholders were all numbered and randomly chosen from a table of random numbers until the five size groups were each filled. Women who declined to be interviewed were replaced by the next random number that fell in that size group.

of social-role differentiation, all show political women with a lesser educational, occupational, and income status than their male counterparts.[34] Analysis of the background data of men and women on the Connecticut councils indicates that although both men and women officeholders are above the median levels of the population, social-role differentiation exists here as well. Table 2 compares the social status of the male and female officeholders with each other and with the general population of the state.

Table 2

Economic/Social Characteristics of Municipal Legislators

Population Characteristics[b]	%Women (n=50)	%Men (n=50)	%Connecticut Population[a]	
Education:[c]				
Less than high school degree	2	0	43.0	
Less than college degree	44	28	42.9	
College degree	38	44	8.1	
Five years more	16	28	6.0	
	100	100	100.0	
Median school years completed	NA	NA	12.2	
Income:[d]				
Less than $10,000	7[e]	0	35.3	
$10,000 to $14,999	13	6	32.5	
$15,000 to $24,999	53	54	23.8	
$25,000 and over	27	40	8.5	
	100	100	100.1	
Median family income (1969)	NA	NA	$12,015	
Occupation:[f]			Female	Male
Professional	26	42	17.4	18.3
Business, Managerial	6	34	3.4	13.0
Clerical, sales, white collar	24	12	45.3	14.8
Skilled, semi-skilled, laborers	2	12	33.9	54.1
Homemaker	42	0	NI[g]	NI
	100	100	100.0	100.2
%in labor force	58	100	43.0	76.6
%not in labor force	42	0	57.0	23.4

aConnecticut data is taken from General Social and Economic Characteristics, U.S. Bureau of the Census, Census of Population: 1970, Vol. 1, Part 8. Data is for white population only (93.5% of the state's population).

bRelationships between males and females in sample:
   Education: Kendall's tau c = .22 (.05).
   Income: Kendall's tau c = .21 (.02).
   Occupation: Cramers' V = .62 (.001).

cData for Connecticut population based upon 1970 figures for whites only, 25 years and over (n = 1,598,715).

dData for Connecticut population based upon 1969 figures for white families only (n = 724,882 families).

en = 45.

fData for Connecticut population based upon 1970 figures for whites in the labor force, 14 years and over (female n = 456,479; male n = 758,022).

gData not included in percentages.

The Occupational Path

        While the women were disadvantaged with respect to education and income, the greatest sex difference appeared in the occupations. The strong association between sex and occupation is largely explained by the number of women homemakers in the sample. Furthermore, the number of male professionals was almost double that of female professionals; also, although not shown in the data, male professionals were mostly lawyers, while women professionals were primarily nurses and teachers. To sum up, while women councilmembers were more educated and had higher family incomes than the average citizens in the state of Connecticut, they suffered in comparison to the male councilmembers with whom they served. Situational and structural explanations for the limited number of women in political office cited earlier point to these comparisons to explain the small number of women in political office: because women are more often housewives and have less education and income than men, they are not able to compete equally

with men for public office.   While these may explain why
so few women achieve political roles, they do not tell how
those who attain office get their positions.   Women appear
to be able to compensate for these deficiencies by using
other means to achieve public office.

The most compelling reason offered for the small
number of women in public office is lack of the qualifications and experiences that accompany certain types of occupations in which men predominate; law and business are
the two most popular occupations among men in office.   They
provide training and contacts to aspiring political elites.
Herbert Jacob's model of elite recruitment cites occupation
as "the crucial social variable" that selects among those
disposed toward political office holding.   "The major factor
is the occupational role an individual plays in his daily life;
the politician emerges only from those roles which teach
him political skills and provide him opportunities to enter
the political arena"[35] (emphasis mine).   Jacob cites placement in a bargaining role as the distinguishing feature of
occupations that are conducive to the development of political careers.   Individuals who must "deal with outsiders
(non-subordinates) and reach a mutually satisfying agreement" are those who can pursue successful political careers.[36]   The importance attributed to such occupational
skills is uniformly emphasized in the recruitment literature.[37]   Even those studies that specifically discuss the recruitment of women to political roles cite the necessity of
particular occupational experiences.[38]   However, among
the women recruited for political office, only a minority
fit the "standard" occupational pattern considered essential.

The Housewife/Volunteer Path

While business and professional women are among
the ranks of political elites (usually in excess of their representation in the population at large), those who study political recruitment, when stressing the importance of certain occupations, generally fail to give adequate attention
to an important source of female political elites.   Studies
show that at least one-third to one-half of the women who
serve as party officials or public officials list "housewife"
as their primary occupation; from the "presidential elite"
at national nominating conventions to state legislators and
local representatives, the housewife is usually the single-
largest classification of occupation for women.[39]   One

exception to the disdain usually afforded the housewife as
a source of female elites is Kirkpatrick's comment in Political Woman. Even this, however, suggests an anamolous
occupational route. "Women legislators have usually been
recruited from a single, deviant, occupation: housewife....
This is an unusual, unfamiliar, sex-specific pathway to political office, one virtually unexplored by political scientists."[40] Merritt suggests it may even be more difficult
for professional women to win election to political office,
since voters are more likely to identify with and support
the "typical" housewife than the professional careerwoman.[41]

       One obvious reason for ignoring this pathway to po-
litical power is the denigration of the housewife role in
American society. The mainstay of the housewife role is
the necessity of bargaining effectively with nonsubordinates
to "reach mutually satisfying agreement." Also, the housewife is almost always in a position where she must compromise with others in order to achieve her objectives: from
the recalcitrant two-year-old or adolescent to the unaccom-
modating service repair companies that force housewives to
fit into their schedules. The abilities to compromise and
bargain are as necessary for an effective housewife as they
are for an effective politician. The possession of certain
personality traits is necessary but not sufficient to propel
women into political office, however. Housewives can become officeholders, but they must compensate for their lack
of occupational skills and training.

       Political women are usually able to follow at least
two alternate routes to public office--the party-volunteer
path or the civic-volunteer path. These are not unique to
women, but they are more important for them, since women
do not have the professional training or business contacts
that men usually have.[42] The major questions to be answered in this study are: what is the path of political recruitment for Connecticut women, and how does it differ
from men's? A preliminary question is: what motivates
women to become political activists when much of their
early socialization militates against it?

Early Socialization to Politics

       One hypothesis often suggested is that women who at-
tain public office are motivated to do so by an early intro-

duction to politics. Many women politicians say politics is
in their blood, having observed relatives and close family members engaged in it. This hypothesis was tested
by looking at the political backgrounds of the local officeholders to see if women differed from men in early
socialization to political activity and if there was evidence
of familial political activity that might account for their
own interest in politics.

One manifestation of early socialization to politics
is discussion of political events at home and exposure
to public officials. Fewer than half the legislators came
from families that discussed politics frequently, and only half themselves discussed politics while they were
growing up; there were no sex differences here. Similarly, there were no statistically significant differences
between the sexes with regard to parents or relatives
holding office. Both men and women officeholders reported a handful of relatives who held public office--
usually a cousin or uncle who held a position in town
government. A small number claimed a father in public office, while none had mothers who ever held a position in government. Table 3, which summarizes the
information on political socialization, indicates that early
exposure to political affairs did not differentiate women
in local government from their male counterparts.

The hypothesis was further tested by looking into the degree and kind of political activity engaged in
by parents. These data are illustrated in Table 4.
Neither men nor women came from families with out-
standing records of political interest and activity: their
parents primarily voted. There were no differences
between the sexes regarding their parents' political behavior.

Part of the early-socialization hypothesis states
that the predominant influence on women politicians is
the mother: that women are drawn to political participation by mothers who serve as role models. [43] The
data do not support this interpretation, since political
participation was dominated by the father in most of
the families--men and women alike. In all cases the
father voted more frequently, discussed politics more
frequently and worked in political campaigns more fre-

Table 3

Political Background of Connecticut Local Representatives

	% Women (n = 50)	% Men (n = 50)	Relationship
Exposure to Politics			
Politics discussed at home:			
Frequently	48	44	n. s.
Not very frequently	52	56	
Own participation in political discussion:			
Frequent	50	50	n. s.
Not very frequent	50	50	
Relative held office:			
Yes	32	18	n. s.
No	68	82	
Father held office:			
Yes	12	6	n. s.
No	88	94	
Mother held office:			
Yes	0	0	n. s.
No	100	100	

Table 4

Parents' Involvement in Politics

	% Women (n = 50)		% Men (n = 50)		Relationship[a]	
Parents' Political Activity[b]	Mother	Father	Mother	Father	Mother	Father
Voted:					n. s.	n. s.
Frequently	86	90	86	92		
Not very frequently	2	4	6	4		
Never	12	6	8	4		
Discussed politics:					n. s.	n. s.
Frequently	24	59	20	42		
Not very frequently	50	33	54	46		
Never	26	8	26	12		
Worked for candidates:					n. s.	n. s.
Frequently	6	20	4	18		
Not very frequently	20	16	22	32		
Never	74	63	74	50		

[a]Refers to relationship between men and women for mother's and father's participation respectively.
[b]Columns for each activity total 100%.

quently than the mother.   Another assumption about political
women is that they become activists through the influence of
working mothers.   Again, the data do not support this theory:
62 percent of the women and 68 percent of the men reported
that their mothers were not employed.   There was no support for the hypothesis that the recruitment of political wom-
en begins at an early age and that early adherence to political
activism enables them to overcome the obstacles that defeat
most women.   The Connecticut women did not get a head
start at home, and they certainly did not follow the example
of mothers who manifested a special interest in political
events, nor were they influenced by mothers playing nontra-
ditional roles.   Clearly, the men were also not overly
influenced by political activism at home; neither sex
seemed to derive much impetus from early socialization
to politics.

The finding that these local women politicians were
not consumed by political affairs all their lives is congruent
with other reports about women in political office.   Most
develop an interest in politics during adulthood, some as recently as the time they are asked to run for office. [44]   In
pursuing the matter of adult socialization, we find that there
was one difference between the sexes that explains more
about the path of female recruitment.   When asked whether
spouses were involved in political activities, 46 percent of
the women and 19 percent of the men (phi=.28, p=.008) reported that their spouse had held public or party office.   An
important agent of political socialization for these women is
not the home in which they grew up but the home in which
they live as adults.   The presence of a politically active
spouse can be a catalyst to a political career for a woman;
men apparently do not have as much need of this sort of
catalyst, for they can assume political roles without it.
Women are able to serve informal apprenticeships before
their entrance into formal political activity because of their
spouses.

Political-Opportunity Structure in Connecticut

Two aspects of the political-opportunity structure have
been discussed.   Political socialization during childhood
seems to have little affect on the recruitment of political
women; it neither encourages them to nor deters them from
seeking office.   The men were not socialized differently.
The situational argument that women do not become politicians

because they lack the occupational training and qualifications
was rejected, since women have proven themselves able to
move from the home into the legislative chamber, especially
at lower levels of office.   What about the structural variables that potentially restrict women's opportunities in public office? Specifically, these variables include political-
party activity, voter prejudice against women public officials,
and family encouragement and support.

Family Encouragement

        Both men and women said they were forced to con-
sider family obligations in their decision to run for office
and were alike in receiving encouragement from family members for their decision to seek office.   Table 5 illustrates
the familial constraints.   Unlike other studies of women in
office, there were no significant differences between the sexes in the ages at which they first ran for office nor in the
number or ages of their children; these women were not
more disadvantaged by family life and home responsibility
than men were.   Both sexes received help from their spouses, and even though they were forced to be away from home
a great deal of time they were confident their spouses understood and accepted the situation.   Contrary to findings
that showed women at higher levels of office must receive
extraordinary support from husbands, these women did not
require special aid and comfort, beyond the fact already
noted that their husbands had themselves been involved in
politics at one time.

        Apparently, the family is not a particular handicap
for women in local office.   The discrepancy between these
findings and others that show women subject to the constraints of family life can probably be explained by the nature of the office the Connecticut women hold.   Local office
is probably the least taxing of political offices; it involves
almost no physical dislocation and can usually be fit into
family schedules without much difficulty.   The other studies
cited were concerned with women in the state legislature,
an office that requires more mobility and more time.

Voter Prejudice

        Female state legislators have noted that voters man-
ifest prejudices about women politicians.[45]   Women politicians,

Table 5

Familial Environment of Local Officeholders

Family Variables	% Women (n=48)	% Men (n=48)	Relationship
Family obligations:			
Were considered in decision to run	64[a]	73[a]	n.s.
Were not considered in decision to run	36	27	
Family encouragement:			
Family encouraged to run	96	89	n.s.
Family discouraged from running	4	11	
Spouse's attitude:			
Spouse positive and supportive	86	77	n.s.
Spouse neutral	13	21	
Spouse negative and nonsupportive	2	2	
Spouse's role:			
Spouse plays a role	60	75	n.s.
Spouse doesn't play a role	40	25	
Politician's absence:			
Away from home a great deal	63	79	n.s.
Not away from home a great deal	38	21	
Age differences when first ran:			
Mean age of running	40	38	n.s.[b]
Mean number of children	3	3	n.s.
Mean age of youngest child	10	8	n.s.

[a]n = 49.

[b]T-Test used for difference of means.

they say, are treated differently from men; they are queried
about their families' approval and their ability to combine
families with political careers. Here, perhaps because of
the nature of the office, politicians reported that voters did
not question women about their family lives more than men.
Furthermore, both men and women also said they felt wom-
en were generally given the same opportunity as men to get
elected or appointed to public office in their communities.
Perhaps the Connecticut women were not subject to greater
intrusion into their private lives because local office is less
demanding than other levels of political office. Perhaps, because they were no longer very young, with young children
at home, there was no need to question them about family
responsibilities. Whatever the reason, these women were
not subject to greater harassment from voters because of
their sex.

So, the discussion has centered around distinctions
between men and women after they made their decisions to
run for office and after they were selected to run under the
party label by the municipal political leaders; there seemed
to be differences in those areas in which women are traditionally at a disadvantage. The analysis will be completed
by examining the political opportunity structure for women
before they are officially sanctioned by the party to run for
office in their communities.

Nominating Criteria

In the state of Connecticut political office holding is
highly dependent upon local-party affiliations, since nomination to state and local office is made by local-party cau-
cuses and conventions. It is important to learn how these
politicians were selected to run for office and what their
community ties were before they received the nod from local-party organizations. Perhaps women are only awarded
the party nomination after serving long apprenticeships in
other offices or living in communities for excessively long
periods of time. Are males sought out and urged to run
by party officials while females are grudgingly allowed to
become party standard bearers? We answered these questions by looking at the number of years each officeholder
spent in the community and the political experience of each.

There were no appreciable differences in the number
of years spent in the town the politicians represented:

twenty-eight years for the men, twenty-five for the women.
Furthermore, this was the first political position for over
three-fourths of these politicians. Of those who had previous political experience, all but one held a position in
municipal government. Most recruited themselves; that is,
they presented themselves as candidates to selection committees.

Women are traditionally the mainstay of political-
party activity; research has shown that they spend more
time on political chores than men do.[46] This involvement
has been found to have important consequences for female
activists; experience in party affairs may compensate wom-
en for less education,[47] may count heavily for them in areas
where competition for office is intense, and may substitute
for occupational ties.[48] It has also been found that women
party elites have been engaged in party activity longer than
the men with whom they share party leadership.[49] The belief is that women require a greater degree of party involvement than men in order to succeed in political office; the
party can at one time represent the greatest impediment as well
as provide the greatest sustenance to politically aspiring women.

The data, illustrated in Table 6, support this hypothesis. There is a relationship between sex and previous
partisan involvement. Additionally, women more frequently
engage in four out of five types of political activity, notably
the routine tasks of political activism; men were only more
active in managing campaigns.

Women can apparently earn their right to become
party nominees by party activism. While men were not
isolated from the political-party network, it appears that
they were able to move into political roles in their communities without spending as much time and energy on party
chores. The men were able to rely upon other resources,
perhaps acquired from their occupations, perhaps from their
political careers; the women were forced to serve apprenticeships in party work before they could assume elite political
roles in their communities.

Summary

Based upon the experiences of these politicians,
party activity appears to be the key to the recruitment
of female local officials. Differences between the sexes
that were found in other political offices were not found
in Connecticut municipal offices. Connecticut women
were not more dependent upon supportive husbands, they

Table 6

Political-Party Activism By Sex

Political Activism	% Women (n=50)	% Men (n=50)	Relationship[a]
Involvement in party politics before office:			
Was involved	80	60	.21 (.04)
Was not involved	20	40	
Political experience:[b]			
Distributed literature			.35 (.001)
Frequently	58	23	
Occasionally	38	65	
Never	5	13	
Contacted voters			.44 (.001)
Frequently	75	32	
Occasionally	25	58	
Never	0	10	
Gave speeches			n.s.
Frequently	38	13	
Occasionally	23	42	
Never	40	45	
Made policy decisions			n.s.
Frequently	33	23	
Occasionally	48	59	
Never	20	23	
Managed campaigns			n.s.
Frequently	25	29	
Occasionally	35	45	
Never	40	26	

[a]Involvement is phi; all other variables Kendall's tau C.

[b]n = 71 for political experience; women = 40, men = 31. Columns for each activity total 100%.

were not older when they initially entered politics, they did
not have fewer children, they did not require greater encouragement from their families before they made the decision to run for office, and they were not forced to consider family obligations more than men were. Furthermore,
they felt they were not subject to prejudice against women
politicians from voters and felt themselves given the same
opportunities as men to become public officials. Men were
not sought out by party officials to run for office; both sexes essentially recruited themselves. Women were not treated differently by party leaders; there was no evidence of
overt prejudice against them or favoritism toward male candidates. Women were not given extra encouragement from
early political socialization into politically active families;
many were not even interested in politics in their youth.
The women were differentiated from their male colleagues
by the impetus they received at home during their adult
lives: their husbands were often involved in public or party
office while the males' spouses were not.

Sex differences found among politicians in higher office were used to guide this study of local public officials.
Most differences found at other levels of office were virtually nonexistent here. Earlier studies of political recruitment of women, as well as most other analyses of women
in politics, focused upon women in state and federal office.
This analysis indicates that generalizations to local office
must be viewed with skepticism. The inability to generalize
may be explained by the fact that local office is qualitatively
different from other types of office; it may be explained by
the importance of the party in Connecticut; it may be due to
individual characteristics of these officeholders. Whatever
the explanation, we suggest the need for further study into
the office that has been most congenial to aspiring women
politicians--the municipal legislature.

Notes

[1]Gabriel A. Almond and Sidney Verba, The Civic
Culture: Political Attitudes and Democracy in Five Nations
(Boston: Little, Brown, 1965).
    [2]Nikki R. Van Hightower, "The Recruitment of Wom-
en for Public Office," American Politics Quarterly 5 (July
1977): 301-314.
    [3]Angus Campbell et al., The American Voter (New
York: John Wiley and Sons, 1964); Lester W. Milbraith,

Political Participation (Chicago: Rand McNally, 1965); and
Sidney Verba and Norman H. Nie, Participation in America:
Political Democracy and Social Equality (New York: Harper
and Row, 1972).

[4]Robert Lane, Political Life (New York: Free Press,
1959); and Campbell et al. , The American Voter; D. Jaros,
Socialization to Politics (New York: Praeger, 1974); and
Fred Greenstein, Children and Politics (New Haven: Yale
University Press, 1965).

[5]Susan Welch, "Women as Political Animals?   A
Test of Some Explanations for Male-Female Political Participation Differences," American Journal of Political Science
21 (November 1977):   711-730; Susan Welch, "Recruitment of
Women to Public Office: A Discriminant Analysis," Western
Political Quarterly, forthcoming, 1978; Kent L. Tedin, David W. Brady, and Arnold Vedlitz, "Sex Differences in Political Attitudes and Behavior: The Case for Situational Factors," Journal of Politics 39 (May 1977):   448-456; Naomi
Lynn and Cornelia B. Flora, "Motherhood and Political Participation: A Changing Sense of Self," Journal of Military
and Political Sociology 1 (March 1973):   91-103; and Anthony
M. Orum, Roberta S. Cohen, Sherri Grasmuck, and Amy
W. Orum, "Sex, Socialization and Politics," American Sociological Review 39 (April 1974):   197-209.

[6]Welch, "Women as Political Animals?" p. 712.

[7]Welch, "Recruitment of Women to Public Office."

[8]Marilyn Johnson with Kathy Stanwick and Lynn Korenblit, Profile of Women Holding Office (New Brunswick: Center for the American Woman and Politics-Eagleton Institute
of Politics, Rutgers University, 1976).

[9]Emily Stoper, "Wife and Politician: Role Strain
Among Women in Public Office," in Marianne Githens and
Jewel L. Prestage, eds. , A Portrait of Marginality (New
York: David McKay, 1977).

[10]Jeane Kirkpatrick, Political Woman (New York:
Basic Books, 1974).

[11]Kent Jennings and Norman Thomas, "Men and Wom-
en in Party Elites: Social Roles and Political Resources,"
Midwest Journal of Political Science 12 (November 1968):
469-492.

[12]Kenneth Prewitt, The Recruitment of Political Leaders: A Study of Citizen Politicians (Indianapolis: Bobbs-
Merrill, 1970); Welch, "Recruitment of Women to Public Office"; and Herbert Jacob, "Initial Recruitment of Elected Officials in the U.S.:   A Model," Journal of Politics 24 (November 1962):   703-716.

[13]Welch, "Women as Political Animals?"; Welch,

"Recruitment of Women to Public Office"; and Jeane Kirk-
patrick, The New Presidential Elite (New York: Russell
Sage Foundation and the Twentieth Century Fund, 1976).
    14Welch, "Women as Political Animals?" p. 728.
    15Kirkpatrick, The New Presidential Elite.
    16Kirkpatrick, Political Woman; Kirsten Amundsen,
A New Look at the Silenced Majority (Englewood Cliffs,
N.J.: Prentice-Hall, 1977); and Susan Tolchin and Martin
Tolchin, Clout: Womanpower and Politics (New York: Putnam's, 1973).
    17Peggy Lamson, Few Are Chosen: American Women
in Political Life Today (Boston: Houghton Mifflin, 1968), p.
26.
    18Albert K. Karnig and B. Olive Walter, "Elections
of Women to City Councils," Social Science Quarterly 56
(March 1976): 608.
    19R. Darcy and Susan S. Schramm, "When Women
Run Against Men," The Public Opinion Quarterly 41 (Spring
1977): 1-12.
    20S. Carroll, "Women Candidates and State Legisla-
tive Elections, 1976: Limitations in the Political Opportunity Structure and Their Effects on Electoral Participation
and Success." Prepared for the Annual Meeting of the American Political Science Association, Washington, D.C., 1977;
Tolchin and Tolchin, Clout: Womanpower and Politics; Van
Hightower, "The Recruitment of Women for Public Office";
and Jennings and Thomas, "Men and Women in Party Elites."
    21Irene Diamond, Sex Roles in the State House (New
Haven: Yale University Press, 1977).
    22Ibid.
    23Jennings and Thomas, "Men and Women in Party
Elites"; and Edmond Costantini and Kenneth Craik, "Women
as Politicians: The Social Background, Personality, and
Political Careers of Female Party Leaders," Journal of So-
cial Issues 28, 2 (1972): 217-236.
    24Paula J. Dubeck, "Women and Access to Political
Office: A Comparison of Female and Male State Legislators," The Sociological Quarterly 17 (Winter 1976): 42-52.
    25Costantini and Craik, "Women as Politicians"; Mar-
tin Gruberg, Women in American Politics (Oshkosh, Wis:
Academia Press, 1968); and Wilma R. Krauss, "Political
Implications of Gender Roles: A Review of the Literature,"
American Political Science Review 68 (December 1974): 1706-
1723.
    26Sharyne Merritt, "Winners and Losers: Sex Dif-
ferences in Municipal Elections," American Journal of Political Science, 21 (November 1977): 731-743; and Karnig and
Walter, "Elections of Women to City Councils."

27Kirkpatrick, Political Woman; Dubeck, "Women
and Access to Political Office"; Diamond, Sex Roles in the
State House; and Emmy Werner, "Women in the State Legislatures," Western Political Quarterly 21 (March 1968): 40-
50.
28Hope Chamberlin, A Minority of Members: Women
in the U.S. Congress (New York: Praeger, 1973); Peggy
Lamson, Few Are Chosen: American Women in Political
Life Today (Boston: Houghton Mifflin, 1968); Werner, "Wom-
en in Congress: 1917-1964"; and F. Gehlen, "Women in
Congress," Transaction 6 (October 1969): 36-40.
29Kirkpatrick, The New Presidential Elite; Jennings
and Thomas, "Men and Women in Party Elites"; and Naomi
Lynn, "Societal Punishment and Aspects of Female Political
Participation: 1972 National Convention Delegates," in Marianne Githens and Jewel L. Prestage, eds., A Portrait of
Marginality (New York: David McKay, 1977).
30Diamond, Sex Roles in the State House.
31League of Women Voters, Connecticut in Focus
(Connecticut Education Fund, 1974), p. 203.
32Ibid., p. 193.
33Prewitt. The Recruitment of Political Leaders: A
Study of Citizen-Politicians, p. 301.
34Costantini and Craik, "Women as Politicians"; Jennings and Thomas, "Men and Women in Party Elites"; Kirkpatrick, The New Presidential Elite; and Dubeck, "Women
and Access to Political Office."
35Jacob, "Initial Recruitment of Elected Officials in
the U.S.," p. 709.
36Ibid.
37Prewitt, The Recruitment of Political Leaders: A
Study of Citizen-Politicians; Lewis Bowman and G.R. Boynton, "Recruitment Patterns Among Local Party Officials: A
Model and Some Preliminary Findings in Selected Locales,"
American Political Science Review 60 (September 1966):
667-676; K. Prewitt and H. Eulau, "Social Bias in Leadership Selection, Political Recruitment, and Electoral Context,"
Journal of Politics 33 (May 1971): 293-315; and Milbraith,
Political Participation.
38Diamond, Sex Roles in the State House; Kirkpatrick,
The New Presidential Elite; Ingunn N. Means, "Women in
Local Politics: The Norwegian Experience," Canadian Jour-
nal of Political Science 5 (September 1972): 365-388; and
Dubeck, "Women and Access to Political Office."
39Stoper, "Wife and Politician"; Means, "Women in
Local Politics"; Diamond, Sex Roles in the State House;
Kirkpatrick, Political Woman; Kirkpatrick, The New Pres-
idential Elite; and Merritt, "Winners and Losers."

[40]Kirkpatrick, Political Woman, p. 61.

[41]Merritt, "Winners and Losers."

[42]Kirkpatrick, Political Woman; and Diamond, Sex Roles in the State House.

[43]Ibid.

[44]Ibid.; and Van Hightower, "The Recruitment of Women for Public Office."

[45]Diamond, Sex Roles in the State House; and Kirkpatrick, Political Woman.

[46]Welch, "Women as Political Animals?"; and Ellen Boneparth, "Women in Campaigns," American Politics Quarterly 5 (July 1977): 289-300.

[47]Dubeck, "Women and Access to Political Office."

[48]Kirkpatrick, Political Woman.

[49]Constantini and Craik, "Woman as Politicians."

RECRUITMENT OF WOMEN TO SUBURBAN CITY COUNCILS: HIGGINS vs. CHEVALIER

Sharyne Merritt

The feminist goal of bringing more women into politics directs attention to political recruitment--who achieves political office and how they get there. The question might be stated: "Do the resources and backgrounds of women in local politics more closely approximate Henry Higgins's ideal of 'a woman being more like a man' or Maurice Chevalier's model of gender-related difference?"

Studies of women legislative and partisan elites at the state and national levels support the Chevalier position in some aspects of recruitment and the Higgins position in others. Although there is some conflicting evidence, these observations indicate two main areas in which the recruitment of women elites differs from that of their male counterparts. First, while men and women elites share some common personality traits, certain studies have found women lacking personality characteristics that may be necessary for political advancement.[1] Second, women are found to be constrained by social roles and lack of resources in ways that men are not.[2] In a third area, however, women are more like men: male and female state and national elites follow similar paths into politics.[3]

86

This paper tests these hypotheses at the local level
by comparing the personality and social and political background characteristics of male and female suburban city
councilmembers. [4] Then, to obtain further insight into the
recruitment process, I examine how these characteristics
relate to political ambition. While it is obvious that serving on a city council is only one of several paths to higher
office, [5] an analysis of the correlates of ambition helps clarify how men's and women's careers differ.

The data for this study come from interviews with
fifty-one women and fifty-one men councilmembers in suburban municipalities surrounding Chicago. Suburban municipalities are of special demographic importance: their residents constituted 37 percent of the U.S. population in 1970.
An analysis of the 120 suburbs in Cook County, Illinois (the
most densely populated of the six counties that make up Chicago Metropolitan Statistical Area), revealed that women
are most likely to be elected in communities with large
populations (chi square = 7.35, df = 3, p < .10) and high median family incomes (chi square = 12.63, df = 3, p < .01). Because of these differences between municipalities with women
legislators and those with all-male boards, only municipalities
with mixed-sex boards were included in the study. I interviewed
fifty-one of the sixty women councilmembers (85 percent) in office as of January 1, 1977. For each woman, a man in the same
municipality with an equal or comparable tenure in office was
interviewed. The sampling procedure thus permitted controlling for community culture, party structure, and experience
in office.

Findings: Sex Differences in Recruitment

Personality Traits. Several personality characteristics were examined. Measures of needs for power, achievement, and affiliation are those used by Jeane Kirkpatrick[6]
in her study of delegates to the National Party Convention.
These measures consist of a series of situational questions
on which respondents rank the relative importance of influence, accomplishment, and friendship. [7] Table 1 shows that
there are no sex differences on these motivational measures.
Men and women are both motivated most strongly by need
for achievement, next most strongly motivated by need for
power, and least motivated by need for affiliation.

Motivation in the sense of incentives was tapped by
an open-ended question: "What aspects of being council-

Table 1

Motivations and Sex

	Men[a]	Women[a]	Relationship[b]
Need for Achievement	63%	65%	n.s.
Need for power	41	41	n.s.
Need for affiliation	10	10	n.s.
(N)			

[a]Percent scoring high (3 or 4). See footnote 5.
[b]Kendall's tau b. Relationship between score on individual
need and sex.

---

member do you like most or find most satisfying?" Responses were grouped according to the four categories developed by Conway and Feigert.[8] These categories are appropriate for this study because they were derived from
open-ended interviews with local officeholders and because
they parallel other typologies of political incentives.[9] Social consists of meeting people and helping people. Personal
includes enjoyment of being in a position of power, being
part of the decision-making process, and learning about
politics. Accomplishment consists of individual achievements
in policy or problem solving.[10] Impersonal subsumes enjoyment from providing services, representing constituents,
and efficiently managing the government.

The data presented in Table 2 indicate that women
are somewhat more likely to cite social incentives and men
to cite accomplishment incentives. At first glance these
findings seem to lend support to the conclusion that more
women than men are motivated by "public-serving considerations."[11] Yet men's and women's comparable citations of
personal (i.e., power) and impersonal (i.e., service) incentives brings this interpretation into question. Further
insight into the social-vs.-accomplishment difference comes
from an examination of the relationships between sex and
needs for power, achievement, and affiliation for each incentive. Women who cite social incentives have lower need
for affiliation scores and higher need for achievement and

Table 2

Incentives and Sex

	Men	Women	
Social	20%	35%	Chi square = 3.51
Personal	20	22	df = 3, p n.s.
Accomplishment	45	35	
Impersonal	14	8	
(N)	(49)	(51)	

need for power scores than men who cite this incentive.
For women, social incentives may be equivalent to accomplishment.   This interpretation fits with the Bardwick and
Douvan suggestion that during adolescence "the establishment
of successful interpersonal relationships becomes the self-
defining, most rewarding, achievement task" for women.[12]

There are also sex differences on two other personality traits: competitiveness and activist orientation.   Competitiveness was measured on a Likert-type scale by a self-
evaluation question.   This is a scale that presents a statement and asks respondents to indicate how strongly they
agree or disagree with the statement.   Fifty-nine percent
of men compared to 30 percent of women describe themselves as "very competitive" (Kendall's tau b = -.27. p < .002.
The relationship between activist orientation and sex is in the
opposite direction.   Women were more likely to agree with the
Likert-type item "I am not satisfied with the world as it is, and
I spend now, and intend to spend, much more of my life trying
to change it" (Kendall's tau b = +.14 p < .05).[13]

Social Resources and Roles.   Studies of state and
national partisan elites suggest that women are "disadvantaged" by their lack of educational and occupational status.[14]
By these criteria, women local elites are similarly disadvantaged.   Women have lower levels of educational attainment than men (Kendall's tau b = -.17 < .05) and are
less likely to have professional or managerial occupations
(Kendall's tau b = -.50 p < .0001).   Table 3 shows that

Table 3

Social Resources and Sex

	Men	Women	Officeholders Men	Women	Relationship[a] (Officeholders)
Education					
Secondary	63%	76%	14%	22%	
Some college	16	13	20	27	
College graduate	11	8	23	29	-.18 p < .02
Postgraduate	10	3	43	22	
(N)			(51)	(51)	
Occupation (all)					
Nonprofessional[b]	c	c	27	76	
Professional	c	c	73	24	-.50 p < .0001
(N)			(51)	(51)	
Occupation (employed)					
Nonprofessional	68	82	26	43	
Professional	32	18	74	57	n. s.
(N)			(50)	(21)	
Family prestige					
Nonprofessional	c	c	26	40	
Professional	c	c	74	60	n. s.
(N)			(50)	(47)	

Population percentages computed from 1970 Census, Summary Tape, Tables 42, 68.

[a]Kendall's tau b.

[b]Including houseworker.

[c]Not provided by Census.

the educational differences in part reflect social patterns in the
population at large. It should be noted, however, that while the
educational composition of both the male and female leadership
samples represents "a systematic distortion" of their respective
subpopulation, [15] the female sample shows greater bias in
leadership selection. Among those with postgraduate education, the ratio of officeholders to subpopulations is 7:1 for
women but only 4:1 for men.

    The relationship between occupation and sex is due
to the fact that over half of the women interviewed were
not employed outside the home. When we control for employment the relationship between sex and occupation is
eliminated; 74 percent of employed men and 57 percent of
employed women have professional or managerial occupations. Again, the bias in leadership selection from the subpopulation is greater for women. Among professionals the
ratio of officeholders to subpopulations is 3.2:1 for women
and 2.3:1 for men. But what of women who are not employed outside the home; how disadvantaged are they?

    Occupation, in addition to facilitating the acquisition
of skills and contacts, [16] is an indirect indicator of economic and social status resources that make political participation possible. Since such resources can be either personal
or acquired from one's family, I included a measure of
family occupational status. I assigned all officeholders the
occupational status of the spouse in their families (whether
that was husband or wife) with the greater prestige. The
lack of relationship between this variable and sex indicates
that women--even nonworking women--are not disadvantaged in
the economic and status resources that permit political activism.

    I hypothesized that women would be more constrained
than men by the demands of their families. In terms of
the presence of children, this does not seem to be the case.
Eighty-eight percent of men and ninety-six percent of women
have at least one child. Although men and women officeholders both have an average of three children, women
were likely to seek office while their children were young.
The average age of youngest child for men at their first
election was eight years old; for women, the average age
was twelve. As such, there is also a sex-related age difference. Women are on an average four years older than
men (male average = forty-four; female average = forty-eight).

    Paralleling Kirkpatrick's findings among convention
delegates, [17] women in this sample are less likely than men

to state that their political activity comes into conflict with their commitments to their families. Thirty-one percent of men but only 6 percent of women perceive their family and political commitments to come into conflict "a great deal." This is not a function of employment status. Employed women are also less likely to report conflict between politics and family. A man's candidacy and/or career can apparently survive any consequent domestic strife. Women, however, are probably less likely to enter or stay in politics if it comes into conflict with their roles as mother and wife. This difference in priority given by men and women to the family is explored by Cynthia Fuchs Epstein in her study of constraints on women. "For women, the obligations attached to family statuses [or roles] are first in priority, while for men the role demands deriving from the occupational status ordinarily override all others."[18] As one woman councilmember stated: "I'm a wife first, a mother second, and an alderman third."

Also paralleling Kirkpatrick's findings, women perceive their spouses to be more supportive of their political activity than men do. Three-quarters of women but only half of men feel that their spouses are "very much in favor of their political activity." This may reflect a greater need on the part of women for encouragement to become involved.[19] It may also reflect different expectations of support. Men may be more accustomed to assistance from their spouses. Discussing the ancillary role of the corporate wife, William Whyte states that management "deliberately plans and creates a favorable, constructive attitude on the part of the wife that will liberate her husband's total energies for the job."[20] Men may, indeed, take this assistance for granted. If this is the case, even a great deal of support may be evaluated as "moderate." Women, on the other hand, less accustomed to help from their spouse, may interpret even a modicum of support as "a great deal."

Recruitment. In her study of convention delegates, Kirkpatrick reports "there were no significant differences in the recruitment of male and female delegates."[21] The data from our local sample partially confirm this finding. There are no differences between men and women in the number of years they have resided in their communities (male average = seventeen years; female average = eighteen years). There are also no differences in whether they were recruited by institutional (mayor, party, or councilmember) or noninstitutional agents (self, friend, relative, or public). Forty-nine percent of men and 57 percent of

women were recruited by institutional agents.   Further,
neither men nor women were likely to have been appointed
to their first office: 82 percent of men and 90 percent of
women were elected.

An interesting difference is revealed, however, when
we look at preelection political bases.   Respondents were
asked about their involvement in a variety of community-
based organizations.   As shown in Table 4, men and women
were equally active in four civic organizations prior to their

Table 4
Community Organizations and Sex

	Men[a]	Women[a]	Relationship[bc]
Church	59%	65%	n. s.
Service	35	30	n. s.
Nonpartisan	51	41	n. s.
Partisan	51	48	n. s.
P. T. A.	33	65	+.31 p .001
League of Women Voters	2	51	+.55 p .0001

[a]Percent officer or very active.

[b]Kendall's tau b.

[c]Relationship between activity in individual organization and
sex.

entry to elective office.   Almost two-thirds of each sample
was involved in church, half of each sample in nonpartisan
and/or partisan groups, and one-third of each sample in
service groups.   Although there are no sex differences in
participation in these four groups, women were also heavily
involved in two additional organizations, PTA (65 percent of
women compared to 33 percent of men) and League of Wom-
en Voters (51 percent of women compared to 2 percent of
men).

Controlling for employment further clarifies the pattern of additional participation for women.   Working women

are equally active in the League of Women Voters but are
less active in the PTA than nonworking women. Since both
groups had school-age children at the time of their first
election, this difference is probably due to the discrepancy
in available daytime hours. Working women are, however,
more likely to be active in church--a community activity
that can take place on the weekend. It seems, then, that
women must have greater civic volunteer experience than
men even if they work. This finding not only confirms previous research, [22] but identifies the character of that sup-
plemental experience. In addition to involvement in mixed-
sex groups, women need a political base in traditionally female organizations--PTA and League of Women Voters. If
they are unavailable for PTA, they must compensate with
involvement in another traditionally acceptable focus for
women--church.

Correlates of Ambition

        Kirkpatrick found among the 1972 delegates "in both
parties, in all candidate groups, and in all age cohorts
women had significantly lower levels of ambition for public
office than men."[23] This forbodes poorly for the future.
It is from the "politically active stratum" that candidates
are recruited.[24] If most women in this stratum do not
aspire to high political office, there will be few potential
women candidates. Thus Kirkpatrick concludes that wom-
en's lower level of ambition offers important clues to contemporary male domination of power processes.[25] Yet
Kirkpatrick's sample was delegates, some of whom were
officeholders, some of whom were party activists, and, of
course, some of whom were both. There was, however, a
relationship between office-holding experience and sex: "In
both parties and all candidate support groups fewer women
than men ... had held public office."[26] The relationship
between ambition and sex, then, might be spurious. It
might actually be tapping a relationship between ambition
and office-holding experience. Although we did not test
this alternative hypothesis with Kirkpatrick's data, our local
sample, comprised of officeholders only, provides an interesting comparison with the findings on delegates.

        Ambition is defined in this study by two questions.
I first asked councilmembers if they planned to seek another
term. Then I asked if they intended to seek a higher office
either immediately after serving as councilmember or in the

future.   Respondents are classified into three groups: those
intending to retire from office, those intending to seek another term, and those intending to seek higher office (corresponding to Schlesinger's three categories, "discrete," "stat-
ic," and "progressive," respectively).[27]   Officeholders who
intend to retire or seek another term and to later seek a
higher office are classified in the third group.   Intention to
seek the same office is defined liberally.   In addition to
those who are certain they will run again, those who are
uncertain about their plans are included within this category.
Since the achievement of high office undoubtedly demands
more intense commitment, however, intention to seek a
higher office is defined conservatively.[28]   Only those who
respond "yes" to the query on higher office are placed in
this group.

Table 5

Career Plans and Sex

	Men	Women	Relationship[a]
Retire	28%	24%	
Seek same office	37	47	n. s.
Seek higher office	35	29	
(N)	(51)	(51)	

[a]Kendall's tau b.

Table 5 presents the distribution of career goals.
Within this sample, ambition is not related to sex.   Furthermore, comparisons of the offices to which ambitious councilmembers aspire (both immediately after serving on the
council and at the top of their careers in politics) reveal
no significant sex differences.   These data are presented in
Table 6.   The hypothesis that women are less politically
ambitious than men is, then, not confirmed at the local
level.

There are, however, sex-related differences in

the plans of those who intend to retire from office. Six-ty-seven percent of women but only 21 percent of men will continue to be involved in the community through volunteer activities. For nonambitious women office holding would seem to be an extension of civic volunteerism. For non-ambitious men it would seem to be a more discrete activity.

Table 6

Office Goals of Those Intending to Seek Higher Office

| | Immediate Plans | | Plans at Top of Career | |
	Men	Women	Men	Women
Mayor	64%	54%	47%	38%
County Officer	0	9	0	0
State Legislature	28	27	33	38
U.S. Legislature	7	9	20	23
(N)	(14)	(11)	(15)	(13)
	Kendall's tau b n.s.		Kendall's tau b n.s.	

Personality Traits. Power and achievement motiva-tion are not related to political ambition for either sex. Need for affiliation is negatively related to ambition for women (Kendall's tau b = -.27 p < .02). Apparently, the more a woman is motivated by a desire for friendship, the less likely she is to seek higher office (women, higher of-fice $\overline{X}$ = .40; women, same office $\overline{X}$ = 1.29; women, re-tiring $\overline{X}$ = 1.17). Although there is no relationship between affiliation and ambition among men, those who intend to con-tinue in the office of councilmember average the highest score on this need (men, higher office $\overline{X}$ = 1.06; men, same office $\overline{X}$ = 1.39; men, retiring $\overline{X}$ = 1.15). The data from both samples, then, lend support to Jeanne Knutson's hypothesis: "The need for affection will propel individuals to seek secure positions ... where factionalism is of minor

importance, in local government, rather than to engage in
the rough and tumble of 'big time' politics. "29

Although there is no relationship between incentives
and ambition for women, a pattern does appear in the data
for men. Men motivated by accomplishment either aspire
to higher office or intend to retire from politics. An analysis of the protocols indicates that some men motivated by
accomplishment see the business world as holding greater
opportunities for personal fulfillment. One says of his satisfactions:

> Most satisfying are the rare times we actually are
> able to instigate a new direction or policy and ac-
> tually carry it out. It's because these times are
> so rare that I'm leaving politics.

Another man describes his greatest rewards as:

> When you get something done and that's where
> I've also had my biggest heartaches and that's
> probably why I'm not running again. I don't
> think you really affect a lot of things and I'm
> a type who's more action oriented. ... I run
> a privately owned business and if I want to do
> something, I do it. That's why I run this kind
> of business and that isn't how government works.

Competitiveness is related to political ambition among
women only (Kendall's tau b = +.30, p < .01). Men are
uniformly competitive: over half at each level of ambition
describe themselves as "very" competitive. Among women,
only the most ambitious describe themselves in these terms.

Activist orientation, however, is related to ambition
for men only (Kendall's tau b = +.25, p < .02). Over
half of the ambitious men strongly or moderately agree that
they are "trying to change [the world]" compared to 42 percent of those intending to remain councilmembers and 21
percent of those retiring from politics. Among women,
however, there is uniformly high agreement with this statement in all groups (60 percent of those seeking higher office, 54 percent of those seeking the same office, and 50
percent of those retiring). It is possible that men with an
activist orientation perceive local politics as a stepping stone
and politics beyond the local level as the place for having
an impact upon public policy. Women may see local politics as a
political sphere in which one can undertake meaningful changes.

Social Resources and Roles. Given the high educational and occupational status of state and national officeholders[30] and the greater mobility of socioeconomic elites,
we would expect social resources to be related to ambition.
This is not the case. Neither education, occupation, nor
family prestige is significantly related to ambition for either
men or women.

Age of youngest child at time of first election and
number of children are also related to ambition for both
men and women. Conflict between political activity and
family commitments is, however, related to ambition among
women. Women who aspire to higher political office cite
greater conflict than their less ambitious sisters. Conflict
between domestic and political roles does not, then, discourage ambition for women. It may be that only women
who are not ambitious view public office as a secondary
commitment that can be accommodated to their families' schedules. As one woman describes her satisfactions:

> I am a mother of four children and a wife and ...
> I find [office] fits in with my lifestyle so well be-
> cause it's close to home. I'm either over at City
> Hall or in the neighborhood so I'm not away from
> my home and family.... I can do my readings,
> studying, and phone calls ... around our family
> life.

Highly ambitious women, though, may view politics as a
profession and therefore a more primary commitment. Ev-
en if the demands made upon ambitious women do not differ
from those of their nonambitious sisters, the interpretation
of the role as "professional," perhaps in part a function of
anticipatory socialization, will lead to conflict. As Epstein
notes, "Persons engaged in professional activity are especially expected to channel a large proportion of their emotional and physical energies into work."[31] The highly ambitious woman, then, has two primary commitments, neither
of which can automatically be accommodated to the other.
Conflict is inevitable. Although men (ambitious and nonambitious alike) also cite family-politics conflict, for them
such conflict may be less likely to have personal or political
repercussions. If the analogy between political career and
professional career is accurate, women are more likely to
experience personal role strain because they (but not men)
have two conflicting priority systems.[32] There are also
possible political repercussions. Epstein points out that the

male professional whose absorption in his work leads to
neglect of his wife and family is "understood" and "forgiven" where as "the lady professional who gives any indi-
cation of being more absorbed in work than in her husband
and family is neither understood nor forgiven."[33] Hence,
the conventional wisdom that voters are more concerned
about the effect of a woman's candidacy on her family than
they are about a man's.

    Recruitment. Political background experiences are
more clearly related to career plans for men than for wom-
en. Ambitious men are less likely to have been appointed
to their first term. One of the seventeen men ambitious
for higher office was appointed to his first term compared
to about a quarter of those who will remain in the same office and two-fifths of those who will retire. Since appointment is likely to be preceded by personal contact with local
influentials it would seem that for men aspiration for higher
office is inversely related to political localism. This interpretation is corroborated by data on organizational participation and recruiting agent. Although there were no relationships between ambition and male participation in five of
the six organizations examined, ambitious men were less
likely to be active in nonpartisan organizations than nonambitious men. Ambitious men are also less likely to have
been recruited by local institutional agents (mayor, party,
or councilmember) and more likely to have been recruited
by noninstitutional agents (self, friend, relative, or public).
Men who are going to stay in the same office or retire from
politics, then, are firmly rooted in local bases. Those who
aspire to higher office are less tied to the community power
structure.

    It is interesting to note that at the election stage a
key to electoral success for male candidates is personal
contact with local politicians.[34] Those recruited by local
institutional agents are most likely to win. What assists
men in local elections, however, is not appropriate for
higher aspirations. The concurrence of local independence
and high ambition for men may help explain why a local apprenticeship is not a prerequisite for a state or national
legislative career.[35]

    The only recruitment variable related to ambition for
women is membership in the League of Women Voters: highly ambitious women are less likely to be active. One possible interpretation of this finding is that for women, too,

aspiration for higher office is inversely related to political
localism.   However, the League of Women Voters is not
purely local.   Many chapters in this area subsume more
than one municipality.   Further, there is interaction between leaders of different chapters and a strong state organization, making it a supralocal political base.   A second
possible explanation is that ambitious women may prefer to
invest their time and effort in projects with which they will
be personally identified rather than those which will be attributed to a group.   A corollary to this view is that ambitious women may not want to be tied to all League (both
local and national) issue positions.   Yet another alternative
interpretation is that the League, by stressing nonpartisan
politics, may inadvertently discourage women from seeking
state or national level office.   Indeed, activity in the League
may become an outlet for political activity that might otherwise be aimed at higher office.   The data from this study
do not permit an evaluation of the relative explanatory power
of each of these interpretations.   However, the position of
the League as a key arena for women to enter the politically active stratum makes its effect on political recruitment
to higher office a concern that should be addressed.

Discussion

        Which model, then--Higgins's or Chevalier's--best
fits the data on resources and backgrounds of women in
local politics?   In terms of personality traits, there is
evidence to support both positions.   There are no sex differences in motivations defined as needs for achievement,
power, and affiliation.   Patterns in incentives (though not
statistically significant) of women citing social themes and
men citing accomplishment, seem to be spurious.   Relationships between incentives, needs, and sex indicate that social
incentives are more strongly tied to achievement needs for
women than for men.   For women, identification of social
incentives would appear to be as indicative of "private serving" considerations as identification of accomplishment incentives is for men.   There are, however, clear sex differences on two personality traits: competitiveness and activist orientation.   Women are less likely than men to describe themselves as competitive and more likely to agree
that they are dissatisfied with the world and are trying to
change it.

        The Chevalier position more consistently applies in

the area of social resources and roles, though, again, with
reservation. Women are less likely than men to have high
levels of educational attainment and occupational status.
There are, however, three important qualifications to this
finding. First, an examination of the occupations of officeholders employed outside the home reveals no significant
difference in occupational statuses of men and women. Second, compared to their respective mass subpopulations, wom-
en are more elite in terms of education and occupation than
are men. Third, on family prestige, an indicator of economic and social status resources that make political participation possible, there are no sex differences.

        The evidence on social roles suggests strong sex dif-
ferences. Women seek political office when their children
are older; are less likely to feel that their political activity
comes into conflict with their family commitments; and perceive their spouses to be more supportive of their political
activity. It is suggested that lack of conflict reflects the
higher priority given to the family by women. Greater
spouse support may indicate a higher need for encouragement or a greater appreciation of help when given.

        Like the state and national studies, the local data
largely support the Higgins position in terms of recruitment.
There are no sex differences in years of residence, recruiting agent, appointment, or participation in church, service,
nonpartisan, or partisan groups. There is, however, one
important exception to the Higgins generalization. Although
women are equally active in these four groups, they are also active in two additional groups, PTA and League of Wom-
en Voters--both of which are traditional female preserves.
If they are unavailable for PTA because of work schedules,
they compensate with greater participation in church--anoth-
er traditionally acceptable focus for women.

        An examination of ambition modifies these conclu-
sions. Among personality traits, ambition is related to
competitiveness for women only and activist orientation for
men only. Thus ambitious women are as competitive as
men and ambitious men are as activist oriented as women.
Similarly, conflict between political and family commitments
is associated with aspirations for women only. It seems
that nonambitious women view political activity as a secondary priority easily accommodated to family demands. Highly
ambitious women view it as a profession and therefore experience role conflict.

Ambition bears more directly upon recruitment for men than women. Several measures suggest that men who are ambitious for higher office are less tied to local power structures than nonambitious men. For women, the only recruitment variable related to ambition is membership in the League of Women Voters. This negative relationship may indicate a decision on the part of ambitious women to be free of time and issue ties to the League, or may denote that activity in the League discourages partisan involvement.

Distinguishing among levels of ambition, then, provides a different view of sex differences. In the two areas where the Chevalier model applied, ambitious women seem more like men. Among the highly ambitious, sex differences in personality are eliminated. Ambitious women are competitive; ambitious men are high in activist orientation. In the area of social roles, ambitious women are as likely to perceive conflict between their political activity and family commitments as are men. In the recruitment area, however, where the Higgins model seems to fit the total sample, ambition reveals gender-related differences.

Among local officials, then, sex differences in personality and roles and sex similarities in recruitment may apply largely to those officeholders who are not ambitious for higher office. Among the ambitious, men and women are similar in personality traits and perception of role conflicts, but will follow different recruitment paths.

Notes

[1]Edmond Costantini and Kenneth H. Craik, "Women as Politicians: The Social Background, Personality, and Political Careers of Female Party Leaders," Journal of Social Issues 28 (1972): 217-236; Bernard Hennessy, "Politicals and Apoliticals: Some Measurements of Personality Traits," Midwest Journal of Political Science 3(November 1959): 336-355; Jeane Kirkpatrick, The New Presidential Elite (New York: Russell Sage Foundation and the Twentieth Century Fund, 1976).

A notable exception is: Emmy E. Werner and Louise M. Bachtold, "Personality Characteristics of Women in American Politics," in Jane Jaquette, ed. Women in Politics (New York: John Wiley, 1974), pp. 75-84. Their data suggest that women state legislators have certain key personality characteristics that facilitate success.

²Costantini and Craik, "Women as Politicians"; Irene
Diamond, Sex Roles in the State House (New Haven: Yale
University Press, 1977); M. Kent Jennings and Norman Thom-
as, "Men and Women in Party Elites: Social Roles and Political Resources," Midwest Journal of Political Science 12
(November 1968): 469-492; Jeane Kirkpatrick, Political Woman (New York: Basic Books, 1974); Kirkpatrick, The New
Presidential Elite; Patricia Kyle, "Socialization and Recruit-
ment Patterns of Women in Party Elite in North Carolina."
Paper presented at the 1974 Annual Meeting of the American
Political Science Association, Chicago, August 29-September
2, 1974; Marcia Lee, "Toward Understanding Why Few Wom-
en Hold Public Office: Factors Affecting the Participation
of Women in Local Politics." Paper presented at the 1974
Annual Meeting of the American Political Science Association,
Chicago, August 29-September 2, 1974; and Emily Stoper,
"Wife and Politician: Role Strain Among Women in Public
Office," in Marianne Githens and Jewel L. Prestage, eds.,
A Portrait of Marginality (New York: David McKay, 1977),
pp. 320-337.
    ³Diamond, Sex Roles in the State House; and Kirk-
patrick, The New Presidential Elite.
    ⁴All respondents were legislators in municipalities.
Although some carry the title "village trustee," some "city
commissioner," and others "city councilmember," the re-
sponsibilities are similar. As such, for convenience, all
will be referred to as "city councilmembers."
    ⁵For a more detailed discussion, see Joseph A.
Schlesinger, Ambition and Politics (Chicago: Rand Mc-
Nally, 1966); and John C. Wahlke, Heinz Eulau, William
Buchanan, and LeRoy C. Ferguson, The Legislative System
(New York: John Wiley, 1962).
    ⁶Kirkpatrick, The New Presidential Elite, Table 12-
8, p. 399.
    ⁷For original items and method of index construction
see Kirkpatrick, The New Presidential Elite, pp. 527, 578.
    ⁸M. Margaret Conway and Frank B. Feigert, "Moti-
vation, Incentive Systems, and Political Party Organization,"
American Political Science Review 62 (December 1968):
1159-1173.
    ⁹For a similar typology, see Peter B. Clark and
James Q. Wilson, "Incentive Systems: A Theory of Organizations," Administrative Science Quarterly 6 (September
1961): 129-166. Conway and Feigert discuss the parallels
of these two classificatory schemes in "Motivation, Incentive
Systems, and the Political Party Organization," p. 1165, fn.
24.

[10]"Accomplishment" is equivalent to Conway and Feigert's "ideological" category.

[11]Costantini and Craik, "Women as Politicians"; Kirkpatrick, Political Woman.

[12]Judith M. Barduick and Elizabeth Douvan, "Ambivalence: The Socialization of Women," in Vivian Gornick and Barbara K. Moran, eds., Women in Sexist Society (New York: Mentor, 1971), p. 230.

[13]Dennis J. Palumbo and Richard Styskal, "Professionalism and Receptivity to Change," American Journal of Political Science 18 (May 1974): 385-394.

[14]Costantini and Craik, "Women as Politicians"; Jennings and Thomas, "Men and Women in Party Elites"; and Kirkpatrick, The New Presidential Elite.

[15]Kenneth Prewitt, The Recruitment of Political Leaders (Indianapolis: Bobbs-Merrill, 1970).

[16]Herbert Jacob, "Initial Recruitment of Elected Officials in the U.S.--A Model," Journal of Politics 24 (November 1962): 703-716.

[17]Kirkpatrick, The New Presidential Elite.

[18]Cynthia Fuchs Epstein, Woman's Place (Berkeley: University of California Press, 1970), p. 98.

[19]Kyle, "Socialization and Recruitment Patterns of Women in Party Elite in North Carolina."

[20]William H. Whyte, "The Wife Problem" in Robert F. Winch, Robert McGinnis, and Herbert R. Baringer, eds., Selected Studies in Marriage and Family (New York: Holt, Rinehart and Winston), p. 188; cited in Epstein, Women's Place, p. 115.

[21]Kirkpatrick, The New Presidential Elite.

[22]Sharyne Merritt, "Winners and Losers: Sex Differences in Municipal Elections," American Journal of Political Science 21 (November 1977): 731-743.

[23]Kirkpatrick, The New Presidential Elite, p. 411.

[24]Prewitt, The Recruitment of Political Leaders.

[25]Kirkpatrick, The New Presidential Elite, p. 413.

[26]Ibid., pp. 428-429.

[27]Schlesinger, Ambition and Politics, p. 10.

[28]Prewitt, The Recruitment of Political Leaders, uses the more liberal definition for his categorizations of both those intending to seek another term and those intending to seek higher office. He notes, however, that his proportions are, as such, inflated.

[29]Jeanne N. Knutson, The Human Basis of the Polity (Chicago: Aldine-Atherton, 1972), p. 44

[30]Donald Matthews, The Social Background of Political Decision-makers (Garden City, N.Y.: Doubleday, 1954);

Donald Matthews, U.S. Senators and Their World (New York: Vintage, 1970); and Samuel Patterson and G. R. Boynton, "Legislative Recruitment in a Civic Culture," Social Science Quarterly 50 (September 1969):   243-264.

31Epstein, Woman's Place, p. 99.

32Although conflict between family and politics is not likely to cause role strain for men because one priority is secondary (family) and one primary (politics), men may experience role strain from conflict between politics and occupation, two conflicting first priorities.   Although we did not query respondents on the degree of occupation-politics conflict they experience several men did volunteer comments on such conflict within the context of the family-politics conflict question.

33Epstein, Woman's Place, p. 100.

34Merritt, "Winners and Losers."

35Schlesinger, Ambition and Politics; and Wahlke et al., The Legislative System.

PART II

Policy Positions and Perceptions
of Organizational Roles

From the perspective of classical democratic theory, citizen participation in all aspects of public decision making is based on a premise that such involvement is essential to the full development of individual potential.[1] In the main, contemporary democrats share in this view and thus would shun the suggestion that women must earn their gains in office holding by demonstrating a gender-based contribution to public affairs. Still, feminists and nonfeminists alike ponder the meaning of increased female participation. Both theoretical and practical concerns motivate reflection on the substantive implication of the shift toward more formal female influence in the policy-making process.

On a theoretical level, scholars speculate on the impact of organizational structure and role forces on behavior of new entrants to a decision-making system. Practical concerns focus more directly on the "will women make a difference?" issue. Here aspirations for a somehow better or at least different insight into both political roles and public policy issues seem to motivate interest and concern. The research questions asked tend to center on two topics: policy positions of female politicians, and perceptions of their organizational roles.

Policy positions of females involved in local policy-making systems are examined from a variety of perspectives. Some researchers simply ask, "What are women's policy

109

concerns?" Others ask, "Do female officeholders uniquely
represent such concerns?" Still others wonder if women
bring a distinctly different perception of public-office holding to public affairs; are their basic attitudes, expectations,
and cognitions different from those of their male colleagues?
Finally, scholars ask, "Do women act in concert to ensure
that certain kinds of issues are brought to the fore and if
so, what patterns of issues result?"

A second set of questions looks at these policy decisions in an organizational setting and inquires into the influence that the organization itself exercises on behavior.
Is there a kind of preoffice-holding experience that some
women officials bring to public service that produces a kind
of convergence of organizational roles and policy orientations?
If so, the increasingly common employment experience of
women may portend neutralization for the future; perhaps
sex distinctions will disappear entirely. How do women officials in predominantly female task groups interact with
staff in promoting a local women's agenda? Might we expect that the same dynamics characterizing behavior in predominantly male groups to hold constant across gender?

Part II of this volume presents research attempting
to answer these questions by focusing on the experience of
political women at the local level. The first paper considers the effect of employment on role behavior and policy orientation of municipal council members. A second paper
examines the impact of feminist attitudes versus organization variables on the policy orientation of female judges.
Two additional papers consider role orientations of female
officeholders. One focuses on local Commissions on the
Status of Women; the other investigates the relationship between numbers of women on local governing boards and perceptions of women in office. A fifth paper considers the
kind of policy agenda produced when women act in concert
on local Commissions on the Status of Women.

In "Sex Differences in Role Behavior and Policy Orientations of Suburban Officeholders: The Effect of Women's
Employment," Sharyne Merritt asks whether women who
work outside the home respond differently to the demands
of office from their counterparts who do not. Analyzing
data from the study of local legislators in suburban municipalities reported in Part I, Merritt finds some support for
the thesis that women's employment neutralizes sex-related
differences in office. Looking first at behavior, she finds

that working women legislators spend the same amount of
time on official business as their male counterparts, and
less than their nonworking female colleagues. As well,
working women are more likely to view constituents as expecting no more from them than they would a man in office.
Next, looking at policy orientations, women's employment
status also has some effect, with working women being more
likely than nonworking women to exhibit interest in physical
and regulatory issues.   Still, work experience does not totally neutralize sex as an explanatory factor; significant differences irrespective of employment status remain in some
areas.

        Beverly Cook, in her article "Women Judges and
Public Policy in Sex Integration," compares the personal
commitment of women judges to feminism and the structural
position of women as tokens as competing explanations for
the various attitudes, including their decision-making propensities on women's issues.   Cook finds feminism useful
in distinguishing cognitions, attitudes, and decisional direction of women judges.   Still, feminism only distinguishes
between greater and lesser positive support for the liberation of ordinary women from traditional roles.   Overall,
women judges in this sample, feminist and nonfeminist alike,
are ahead of public opinion in support from women's liberation.   Proportionality, the number of women serving on a
bench, is less useful in understanding women judges' views
on policy questions.   For example, in making simulated decisions in three areas of potential sex discrimination, the
structural condition of number explains no difference in the
decision making of female judges.

        In "Organizational Role Orientations on Female-Dom-
inant Commissions: Focus on Staff-Commission Interaction,"
Debra W. Stewart examines the thesis that staff dominance
is neither an inevitable correlate of effective organization,
nor a sign of organizational malady.   The thesis is explored
through an examination of commissioner-staff relationships
on five reputedly successful Commissions on the Status of
Women (CSW).   Stewart finds that dominance of staff over
board is not an inevitable correlate of success.   In four of
the five commissions certain resources commissioners bring
to commission tasks and special circumstances in the life
of the commission strengthened board vis-à-vis staff.   As
well, the cases studied lend support to the hypothesis that
boardmember attitudes toward sharing control with the staff
are positively related to staff-commissioner agreement on

the goals of the commission. In general, recent findings
about board-staff relationships on predominantly male boards,
or on evenly balanced boards, gain support with the female
dominant commission boards as well.

In an article by Susan Gluck Mezey, "Perceptions
of Women's Roles on Local Councils in Connecticut," the
data on local-office holders in Connecticut, reported in
Part I, are looked at from a different angle. This article not only explores sex differences in perceptions of
women's roles in local political office but also investigates
the effect of numbers of women serving together on local
municipal councils on the attitudes toward women officeholders. Perceptions of women's roles are divided into four
categories: equal opportunity for women in public office,
social integration of women in politics, personality differences between men and women politicians, and representation of female constituency by women in public office. Although Mezey finds sex differences on all four dimensions,
some of them significant, she finds no relationship between
various measures of numbers of women serving together
and perceptions of women's roles.

In the final paper in Part II, "Commissions on the
Status of Women and Building a Local Policy Agenda," Debra W. Stewart adopts an agenda-building perspective to analyze female participation as expressed through local Commissions on the Status of Women. Stewart reports support
for the hypothesis that issues appear on commission agenda
with varying frequency, with issues manifesting potentially
greatest subgroup appeal appearing most frequently. Support also emerges for the hypothesis that issues reflecting
a narrow appeal cluster together. Stewart proposes that
such issue clusters invite support from a variety of subgroups.

The findings presented in Part II begin to provide
some early answers to the question: What difference does
it make when women become active in local decision making? One obvious difference is that when their activity is
channeled into a Commission on the Status of Women, a
women's agenda emerges. Yet as Stewart's article points
out, the shape of that agenda might be restricted by the
ease with which some issues tap traditional values. But
beyond simply introducing new issues, differences can
emerge in how these female politicos see their roles, in
what values they hold, and in how they organize themselves

for action.   The articles to follow bring significant new insights on all these matters.

Mezey and Merritt both find significant sex differences on policy positions and role perceptions of local-office
holders.   Thus their work suggests that, beyond the generally salutary effect increased participation of any group has
on a political system, women in office actually bring about
a new way of looking at issues and representing the constituency.   This latter finding is somewhat modified by Merritt's conclusion that several significant differences disappear
if you compare only women with work experience to their
male counterparts.   Going beyond the simple question of
biological identification with the female sex, Cook's finding
that commitment to feminism explains significant difference
in women judges' attitudes and policy predispositions holds
yet deeper implications for the "do women make a difference?" discussion.   It suggests that a qualitative consideration should be introduced into the effort to increase female
office holding with stress on aspirants with feminist credentials.

Turning to how the officeholders are influenced by
their organizational environment, we see that two of the
articles, those by Cook and Mezey, show little support for
the very prominent thesis that the number or proportion of
women versus men in a decision-making peer group influences various aspects of members' behavior and cognitions.
This finding may point toward either a revision of Rosabeth
Moss Kanter's[2] proportions theory or toward more extensive testing of the theory in larger political decision-making
units.   Stewart, by way of contrast, finds support in the
case of female-dominant decision-making bodies for a thesis
popular in the broader literature on board-staff relationships.
The broader literature suggests that conflict is not necessarily bad and that consensus may be a natural by-product
of a priori agreement.

The articles in this section hold in common focus the
question: "Does sex make a difference?"   To be sure, these
essays cannot promise definitive answers to that question
with respect to either policy positions women officeholders
assume or perceptions held of their organizational roles.
Still, the articles to follow do provide some sound partial
answers; perhaps more importantly they advance an ever
stronger and sharper statement of those questions at the
local level.

Notes

[1]For the clearest recent statement of this premise, see Peter Bachrach, The Theory of Democratic Elitism (Boston: Little, Brown, 1967).

[2]Rosabeth Moss Kanter, "Some Effects of Proportions on Group Life: Skewed Sex Ratios and Responses to Token Women," American Journal of Sociology 28 (March 1977): 965-990.

SEX DIFFERENCES IN ROLE BEHAVIOR AND POLICY
ORIENTATIONS OF SUBURBAN OFFICEHOLDERS:
THE EFFECT OF WOMEN'S EMPLOYMENT

Sharyne Merritt

The historically dramatic increase in women's participation
in the labor force during the past quarter-century is both
a cause and consequence of wider social changes, with repercussions experienced well beyond the economic sphere.
Much has been made of the effect of this participation on
family roles and structure.[1] Some attention, too, has been
given to employment experience's effect on women's assumption of public roles. Two early findings merit note: working women are more likely to vote[2] and women convention
delegates who work hold less idealized views of political
processes.[3] These relationships suggest that specific public roles women increasingly choose to play may be influenced by working.

At least three potential effects of employment may
influence the political participation of both men and women:
verbal and technical skills, increased self-esteem, and increased involvement in voluntary organizations. It is commonly assumed that lawyers have mediation and conciliation
skills that are particularly relevant for state- and national-
level legislative office. Prewitt notes, however, that busi-

ness and accounting are appropriate to local council positions and that "the channels leading to council positions are
dominated by local businessmen."[4] Self-esteem, too, re-
lates to political participation. Jeanne Knutson shows that
individuals with higher levels of esteem feel more able to
influence the government.[5] Third, employment provides access to unions and professional associations. Membership
in such organizations influences sense of political competence, discussion of politics, and breadth of political opinion.[6]

     Two additional effects of employment are especially
relevant to the political participation of women. First, by
providing adult-centered rather than child-centered interaction, employment can increase the scope of women's politically relevant attitudes and associations.[7] Second, employment may heighten sensitivity to sex discrimination in hir-
ing, salary, and promotion, which in turn is related to political liberalism.[8]

     In this study we look at the effect of work experience
among municipal-office holders. The question is, do wom-
en who work outside the home respond differently to the demands of office from their counterparts who do not? This
study of municipal-office holders suggests that work experience may make a difference and that the difference hinges
on the fact that the skills and resources working women
bring to office resemble more closely those of male officeholders. If work experience does render female officeholders more like their male colleagues, the point is not that
being more like men is necessarily an absolute advantage.
However, skills acquired in the male-dominated work world
may permit women to compete more effectively in these public positions and thus more effectively bring their own female perspectives to bear on public policy. As a frame of
reference within which to interpret the effect of women's
work on office holding, we will first examine sex differences
between men and women officeholders in terms of both their
behavior in office and their policy orientations. Then we
will see how women's employment experience affects these
relationships.

Methodology

These issues were examined through a survey of legislators
(councilmembers, trustees, and commissioners) in suburban

municipalities surrounding Chicago.   Suburban municipalities
are of special demographic importance: their residents constituted 37 percent of the U. S. population in 1970.   An analysis of the 120 suburban villages and cities in Cook County,
Illinois (the most densely populated of the six counties that
make up the Chicago Metropolitan Statistical Area), revealed
that women are most likely to be elected in communities
with large populations (chi-square = 7.35, df = 3, p < .10)
and high median family incomes (chi-square = 12.63, df =
3, p < .01).   Because of these differences between municipalities with women legislators and those with all-male
boards, only municipalities with mixed-sex boards were included in the study.   I interviewed fifty-one of the sixty
women municipal legislators (85 percent) in office as of
January 1, 1977.   For each woman, a man in the same
municipality with an equal or comparable tenure in office
was interviewed.   The sampling procedure thus permitted
controlling for community culture, party structure, and experience in office.

    Although the respondents are drawn from only one
county, an analysis of previous surveys suggests that councilmembers in suburban Cook County may be similar in
terms of personal characteristics and political environments
to councilmembers in comparably sized municipalities throughout the nation.   A study of a national sample of councilmembers (n = 512; population under 100,000 subsample, n =445)
was conducted by the National League of Cities in 1973;[9] a
similar study of the population of councilmembers in suburban Cook County was conducted in 1975 (response rate =
61 percent; n= 468).   Kolomogorov-Smirnov two sample
tests indicate no significant differences in age or level of
education between Cook County councilmembers and those
in other cities of under 100,000.   There are also no differences in sex distributions (90 percent of the Cook County
respondents and 91 percent of the national subsample are
male) or partisan activism (39 percent of the Cook County
councilmembers and 41 percent of the national subsample
were active in partisan groups before their election).   Only
with respect to income do the two samples differ: Cook
County councilmembers tend to have higher family incomes
than those in other small cities (D = .338; p < .001).

    The political milieux are also similar.   Both the
National League of Cities survey and the Cook County Study
included lists of issues and asked respondents to indicate
which were most important.   Rank ordering of the nine

issues listed in both instruments is identical with the exception of a lower interest in waste treatment in Cook County. These findings suggest that the Cook County respondents
do not come from an idiosyncratic population. Therefore,
the conclusions drawn from this study may be generalizable
beyond this geographical setting.

Findings: Behavior in Office

Increasing the participation of women in electoral
politics is, of course, one of the aims of women's movement. In addition to the long-term goal of providing nontra-
ditional role models, bringing women into politics is expected to have two immediate effects on the conduct of government. First, women may have an impact on the day-to-day
functions of government by providing new interpretations of
officeholding. Given traditional feminine socialization to
be nurturant and to serve other, we might expect women
officeholders to be more responsive to constituents. We
might also expect women to infuse politics with a more interpersonal, less instrumental style. Second, women may
affect politics by supporting "feminist" policy positions.
Thus, increasing the number of women in office would result in more legislation directly aimed at "women's issues"
and sexual equality.

Our first question then is, do women in local office
act differently from men? To answer this question, I examined five aspects of behavior in office: number of hours
spent on matters related to office, number of constituents
seen on a one-to-one basis, perception of constituent expectations, role orientations, and perceptions of influence on
board decisions.

Table 1 presents comparisons between variables related to behavior in office for men and women and for working and nonworking officeholders. The first column shows
the relationship between each type of office behavior and
sex. The second column uses data from only employed
men and women and again presents relationships between
behaviors and sex. The figures in the first two columns,
then, describe how different men and women are. A positive correlation indicates that women score higher on the
trait; a negative correlation indicates that men score higher;
and no significant correlation ("n.s.") indicates that men and
women score very similarly and that any difference can

Table 1

Behavior in Office

	Relationship with Sex (total sample)	Relationship with Sex (employed sub-sample)	Relationship with Employment (women only)
Number of hours per week	+.18 p<.05*	n.s.*	-.24 p<.05*
Number of constituents per month	n.s.*	n.s.*	n.s.*
Constituents expect more from (man/woman)	+.16 p<.05*	n.s.	n.s.
Constituents trust (man/woman) more	+.37 p<.0001	+.32 p<.002	n.s.
Process/Produce orientation	+.20 p<.03	+.18 p<.05	n.s.
Amount of influence	n.s.	n.s.	n.s.

*Pearson's r. All other coefficients are Kendall's tau b. A positive correlation on a relationship with sex indicates higher scores for women. A positive correlation on a relationship with employment indicates higher scores for employed women.

probably be attributed to chance alone. The figures in the third column represent the relationships between behaviors and employment for women only. That is, it documents whether working and nonworking women officeholders differ. In this case a positive correlation indicates higher scores for employed women; a negative correlation indicates higher scores for unemployed women; and no significant correlation ("n.s.") indicates little difference between the two groups.

The positive correlation between "number of hours per week" and sex (+.18) shows that women as a group spend more time on matters related to the functions of their office. On the average, women spend seventeen hours per week, while men spend an average of fourteen hours per week. Since the councilmember's position is part-time, we should expect regular employment of councilmembers to be a key factor determining the amount of time officeholders invest in their position. Indeed, when we compare working women and men (all but one of whom currently work outside the home), as Table 1 reflects, there is no difference in the number of hours devoted to office activity. Each group averages fourteen hours a week. An additional finding, not reflected in Table 1, is instructive with respect to female-officeholder time expenditure. Although working women do not put as many hours into their occupations as men do (working women $\overline{X}$ = 34, men $\overline{X}$ = 47.5 hours per week), they do spend at least twenty hours more per week than men on household tasks. The net effect of these time expenditures indicates that working women contribute proportionately more time than men to political activity. Not unexpectedly, women who do not work outside the home spend the most time on official business--an average of nineteen hours per week.

The overall sex difference in time spent on office activity does not hold true with respect to number of interactions with constituents. On this variable Table 1 indicates no significant sex differences. Each sex deals with an average of thirty constituents on a one-to-one basis per month. The pattern for men and working and nonworking women does, however, reflect the time expenditures discussed above: with working women seeing an average of twenty-six constituents and nonworking women an average of thirty-two constituents per month. It may be that more constituents come to nonworking women because they trust a "traditional" woman more than a "career" woman or because they perceive nonworking women to be more available.

The responses to two questions about perceptions of constituents help clarify which of these perceptions--trust or availability--best explains the differences in number of constituent interactions. When asked about constituents' trust, both working and nonworking women are more likely than men to agree that constituents trust them more than they would a member of the other sex (women were asked if constituents trust them more than they would a man; men were asked if constituents trust them more than they would a woman). If this reflects a stereotype of women being more ethical than men, it applied equally to "traditional" and "career" women. In the words of one woman councilmember:

> People think women are more honest. I don't
> see why they should, but that's the general as-
> sumption. No matter who you are, if you're a
> woman people just assume you won't lie.

With respect to availability, responses to a question about constituent's expectations suggest that only nonworking women think their sex affects constituents' demands: they are more likely to agree that constituents expect more from them than they would a man. (Men were asked if constituents expect more from them than they would a woman.) It is possible that constituents place greater demands on nonworking women--at least in terms of contacting them-- because they, in fact, are more available, not because constituents regard them to be more trustworthy, i. e., in terms of traditional feminine role expectation. As one woman councilmember puts it,

> People call me because they know I'm here [at home] during the day--even people from outside my ward. They don't call the other aldermen because they're at work and no one wants to disturb them. But since I'm usually at home during the day everyone calls me with their problems.

The next behavioral variable, role orientation in office, is defined as satisfactions from office. We asked respondents, "From which of these two aspects of the job of councilmember do you gain the most satisfaction? Participating in processes such as negotiating and dealing with colleagues or achieving concrete end-products such as services or construction." What we found contradicts expectations derived from theory about sex-linked expressive/instrumental role dimension. That theory asserts that women specialize in social/emotional activities and men specialize in task or means-end activities. We found men more likely to cite satisfactions from processes such as negotiating and women to cite satisfactions from producing concrete end-products. And women's employment status did not alter this relationship. We can invoke three possible explanations to interpret these women's apparent departure from the traditional expressive role, in which women are assumed to get less satisfaction from the more instrumental product/goal achievement than from the more expressive negotiating process.

First, the lack of socialization experiences that premium bargaining/negotiating and other related skills that boys more routinely get from participation in team sports may explain this effect. Boys learn how to maintain intragroup relations through team participation. Girls play games that do not foster competitive skills or encourage capacity to tolerate associations with nonintimates. Henning and Jardim[10] suggest that these may be reasons why women in management often fail to exhibit such critical interpersonal skills as influence, tolerance, cooperation, and discretion in lateral relationships.

Still another socialization effect that may contribute to these women's unexpected source of role satisfaction is training "to help others," that is, traditional femininity's injunction "to be of service." Perhaps they view the accomplishment of concrete goals as more public serving and negotiation as more private serving. Perhaps, in other words, they need to see concrete accomplishments as satisfactions from serving others and negotiations as preparatory acts that seem more to serve personal career goals.[11]

A third possible explanation for women's product orientation hinges on previous history with sex discrimination. Women may reject negotiation with colleagues because they have been systematically excluded from the informal arenas in which negotiations take place.

The final behavior variable is influence on the board. Although there are no sex differences in the amount of influence men and women perceive they have on board decisions, they do differ in terms of what they see as the source of their influence. Employed women cite sources of influence more like the ones men do. Henning and Jardim[12] report that women in management cite passive reasons for success: "It just happened," "I was just lucky," "I was dragged kicking and screaming up the ladder." The data presented in Table 2 suggest that a similar pattern exists in local government. One-fifth of the women see sex, i.e., "being a woman," as the key factor determining their amount of influence. They note that their opinions are either valued because "as a woman" they have a "unique perspective" or they are devalued because as women their views are considered "unimportant." One typical response was: "I'm gaining more influence now but it's been a real struggle because I'm a woman." Another quarter cite organizational structure (e.g., member of majority party, all councilmembers have equal influence). "Our form of government gives everyone an equal amount of influence. We have a cooperative council that listens to everyone's views." Almost half cite either preparation or expertise (both of which are active because they require the application of personal skills). "I do my homework," "I'm an accountant so they turn to me for financial advice." By comparison, a quarter of the men cite persuasiveness, a skill requiring active self-involvement,

but only three women do so.   Employed women, more like
these men, cite expertise and persuasiveness as sources of
influence.   Both sex and employment then seem to affect how
women perceive their influence.

Table 2

Reasons Cited for Level of Influence

	Men	Women (all)	Working Women	Nonworking Women
Sex	0%	22%	21%	22%
Expertise	33	13	21	7
Preparation	14	33	32	33
Organization of board	29	26	10	33
Persuasive- ness	24	6	16	4

Relationship with sex (total sample) Chi square = 20.7,
$p < .0005$

Relationship with sex (employed sub-sample) Chi square =
14.2, df = 4, $p < .01$

Relationship with employment (women only)   n.s.

Policy Orientations

        As noted above, policy orientations of women of-
ficeholders are important within the context of the women's
movement.   Proponents of increasing women's political participation anticipate that women will bring more "feminist"
orientations to government.   Is that the case at the local
level?

        In this study policy orientations measured were

self-identified liberalism/conservativism, positions on women's
issues, and issue priorities. Table 3 presents the relationship
between these variables and sex, including control for employment.

Table 3

	Relationship with Employment (women only)	Relationship with Sex (employed sub sample)	Relationship with Sex (total sample)
Liberalism/ conservatism	n. s.	n. s.	n. s.
Women's Issues			
SHARE	n. s.	n. s.	n. s.
ACHIEVER*	n. s.	+.23 p<.002	+.26 p<.005
WOMEN EXECU- TIVES	n. s.	+.36 p<.001	+.36 p<.001
QUEEN BEE	+.22 p<.04	+.33 p<.001	+.27 p<.001
Issue Specialization			
Most important issue facing municipality	n. s.	n. s.	n. s.
Most interesting issue	n. s.	n. s.	+.19 p<.05

*Item responses reversed, so a positive correlation on a rela-
tionship with sex indicates a more feminist response by women
and a positive correlation with employment indicates a more
feminist response by working women.

The distributions of men and women on the liberal/con-
servative spectrum are almost identical, and women's employment status does not affect the relationship. In spite of this general ideological similarity, however, women are more liberal
on women's issues. We examined three such issues by asking
respondents how much they agreed or disagreed with a series of
statements. Attitude toward changing domestic roles was measured with the statement: "men should share work around the
house with women, such as doing the dishes, cleaning, and so
forth" (SHARE).[13] Role changes in the public domain were
measured with two items: "It is better for everyone involved
if the man is the achiever outside the home and the woman takes

care of the home and family" (ACHIEVER); and "Women should
be considered as seriously as men for jobs as executives or
politicians or even President" (WOMEN EXECUTIVES).[14] At-
tribution of the disadvantaged status of women to societal rather
than individual factors was measured with the statement: "Most
women have only themselves to blame for not doing better in life"
(QUEEN BEE).[15]

Men and women are equally supportive of changing
domestic roles. Sex is, however, related to responses to
public-domain items (ACHIEVER and WOMEN EXECUTIVES):
women give more feminist responses. These findings of
men's lower support for changes in the public as compared
to private sphere are consistent with the results of other
studies.[16] Women are also less likely to agree with the
QUEEN BEE item. Unlike the successful women studied
by Staines, Tavris, and Jayarantne,[17] women local political
elites see the lack of success of most women as a product
of institutional sexism. Women's greater support for changes
in public roles is thus indicative of a general sensitivity to
the women's movement rather than merely a reflection of
their own personal stake in public domain equality.

It is interesting to note, though, that among women
there is a significant relationship between the QUEEN BEE
item and employment. Working women are less likely to
be QUEEN BEES. This may be due to personal experience
with employment or salary discrimination or to other work-
place interactions that expand their experiences beyond the
isolation of the home.[18]

The final set of questions on policy orientations tapped
the matter of issue priorities. Issue priorities are defined by two items: first, the most important issue perceived to be facing the municipality, and second, the issue
area respondents found most interesting. To assess differences in issue priorities, responses were grouped into two
categories: social issues (including integration, public safe-
ty, youth, senior citizens, recreation, and personnel) and
physical or regulatory issues (including public works, long-
and short-term planning, commercial and industrial development, and technical or legal matters). There is no relationship between sex and perception of the most important
issue facing the respondent's municipality. It may be that
problems in the communities are so well articulated (or so
limited) that there is general agreement on which are most
pressing. There is, however, some sex-related issue

specialization in areas of personal interest.   Although both
men and women are most interested in physical or regulatory areas, women are more likely to express an interest
in social topics.   Thirty-five percent of women compared
to 18 percent of men cite a social issue as most interesting.
But this is not true for working women, who are no more
likely to express an interest in social issues than are men.
Apparently, the greater appeal of social issues to women
is less a function of traditional sex-role socialization than
it is of home-centered experience.   Perhaps the centrality
of domestic and familial problems in the lives of nonworking women carries over into their councilmember roles.

Discussion

Sex does distinguish certain aspects of behavior in
office but women's employment neutralizes some of these
sex-related differences.   As we have seen, women spend
more time on matters related to their office, perceive that
their constituents both trust and expect more from them
than they would a man, prefer getting things done to negotiating, and are more likely to attribute their levels of influence on board decisions to passive than to active sources.
When we look at these relationships for employed women
we see that: 1) working women spend the same amount of
time on official business as men (and less time than nonworking women), and 2) working women are likely to view
constituents as expecting no more from them than they
would a man in office.   This suggests that constituents correctly assess working women's level of availability.

Sex is also related to policy orientations, and, again,
women's employment status has some effect.   While officeholders of both sexes are likely to support changing domestic sex roles, women are more supportive of women's
changing roles in the public domain.   Women are also more
interested in social issues than men are.   Women's work
experience does affect the way they view issue priorities:
they are more likely than nonworking women to be interested
in physical regulatory issues.

Sex does make a difference, then, in interpretations
of public office.   But to what extent are these differences
due to sex-role socialization and to what extent to employment?   Three sex differences disappear when we control
for employment: number of hours spent on official matters,

perceptions of constituents' expectations, and issue specialization. One other sex difference--attribution of influence to
passive or active sources--is less noticeable within the employed subsample, though it remains significant.

Hours spent on council duties and constituent expectations would both seem to be related to availability. Issue
interests and sources of influence, it will be recalled, both
related to expertise. It appears that employment blurs sex
differences in two ways. First, it limits the amount of
time working women (like working men) have available for
office-holding activities. Second, it provides women with
comparable professional skills to be applied to political
roles.

Three sex differences remain when employment is
controlled: role orientation (negotiating vs. products), perceptions of citizen trust, and public-domain feminism. The
relationships of sex with role orientation and citizen trust
may be due to differences in either socialization or political
experience. Women's preference for "achieving concrete
end-products" rather than "negotiating with colleagues" may
reflect a lack of childhood team-sport experience or a "public serving" view of government that is compatible with traditional female role expectations. Women's choice of this
"product" style may also be a consequence of experience
with discrimination: they may reject dealing with colleagues
because they are denied access to interpersonal networks in
which negotiations take place. Similarly, women's assess-
ments of constituents' trust could be traced to either sex-
role socialization or office experience. Constituents' perceptions of women as more trustworthy than men (whether
this is an accurate evaluation of public sentiment or a pro-
jection of women respondents' self-images) could derive from
traditional views of feminine morality. Alternatively, such
perceptions could reflect women's lack of experience in positions of power, with the implication that as women gain
greater access to the "means of corruption" they may be
perceived as men are.

The convergences between working women and men
in public office suggest that as women continue to enter the
work force and as women gain more experience in politics,
we are likely to see their behavior differing less and less
from that of men. In the short run, however, women's
feminist orientations, enjoyment of getting things done, and
perceived trustworthiness, in addition to nonworking women's

greater availability and social-issue specialization, may provide unique contributions to the political system.

Notes

[1]Ann H. Stromberg and Shirley Harkess, Women Working: Theories and Facts in Perspective (Palo Alto, Calif.: Mayfield, 1978).

[2]Kristi Andersen, "Working Women and Political Participation, 1952-1972," American Journal of Political Science 19 (August 1975): 439-453; and Susan Hansen, Linda Franz, and Margaret Netemeyer-Mays, "Women's Political Participation and Policy Preferences," Social Science Quarterly 57 (March 1976): 576-590.

[3]M. Kent Jennings and Norman Thomas, "Men and Women in Party Elites: Social Roles and Political Resources," Midwest Journal of Political Science 12 (November 1968): 469-492.

[4]Kenneth Prewitt, The Recruitment of Political Leaders: A Study of Citizen Politicians (Indianapolis: Bobbs-Merrill, 1970), p. 161.

[5]Jeanne Knutson, The Human Basis of the Polity: A Psychological Study of Political Man (Chicago: Aldine-Atherton, 1972), pp. 213-214.

[6]Gabriel A. Almond and Sidney Verba, The Civic Culture: Political Attitudes and Democracy in Five Nations (Boston: Little, Brown, 1965), pp. 252-255.

[7]Naomi Lynn and Cornelia Butler Flora, "Motherhood and Political Participation: A Changing Sense of Self," Journal of Military and Political Sociology 1 (Spring 1973): 91-103.

[8]Wilma McGrath and John Soule, "Rocking the Cradle or Rocking the Boat: Women at the 1972 Democratic National Convention," Social Science Quarterly 55 (June 1974): 141-150.

[9]Raymond Bancroft, America's Mayors and Councilmen: Their Problems and Frustrations (Washington, D.C.: National League of Cities, 1974).

[10]Margaret Henning and Ann Jardim, The Managerial Woman (Garden City, N.Y.: Anchor Press, 1977).

[11]Jeane Kirkpatrick, Political Woman (New York: Basic Books, 1974); and Naomi Lynn and Cornelia Butler Flora, "Societal Punishment and Aspects of Female Political Participation: 1972 National Convention Delegates," in Marianne Githens and Jewel L. Prestage, eds., A Portrait of Marginality (New York: David McKay, 1977).

12Henning and Jardim, Managerial Woman, p. 7.

13Karen Mason, John Czajka, and Sara Arber, "Changes in U.S. Women's Sex Role Attitudes, 1964-1974," American Sociological Review 41 (1976): 573-596.

14Ibid.

15Graham Staines, Carol Tavris, and Toby Epstein Jayaratne, "The Queen Bee Syndrome," Psychology Today 7 (January 1974): 55-60.

16Marie Withers Osmond and Patricia Yancey Martin, "Sex and Sexism: A Comparison of Male and Female Sex Role Attitudes," Journal of Marriage and Family 37 (November 1975): 744-758; Sharyne Merritt and Harriet Gross, "Women's Page Editors: Does Sex Make a Difference?" Journalism Quarterly, forthcoming.

17Staines, Tavris, and Jayaratne, "Queen Bee."

18Cornelia Butler Flora, "Working-Class Women's Political Participation: Its Potential in Developed Countries," in Githens and Prestage, eds., A Portrait of Marginality.

WOMEN JUDGES AND PUBLIC POLICY IN SEX INTEGRATION

Beverly Blair Cook

Women on the bench, like women in legislatures, executive offices, and party organizations, find themselves in a distinct minority. Only 4 percent of judges with law degrees are female. It seems reasonable that the token status of women on the courts would bear some relationship to their attitudes and behaviors.[1] Very little is known about women judges.[2] Until recently only case studies were feasible, since too few women served on major trial courts to provide data for quantitative analysis. One purpose of this paper is simply to describe some characteristics of women on general-jurisdiction courts. The second purpose is to relate some of their cognitions, attitudes, and decision-making propensities to structural and personal variables.

Models used to explain the limited number of women in authoritative positions have employed two types of variables in separate studies: personal level, described by female characteristics, socialization, and attitudes;[3] and systemic level, described by cultural and organizational constraints.[4] By employing both types of variables in the same study, we can examine the relative utility and the interrelationship of personal and systemic variables.[5]

Although we have some understanding of sex discrimination in the selection of women for political office, [6] we
still know little about the decisions made by women in public office. [7] In particular we do not know whether women
(or other minorities) play a representative role by using
their authority to break down traditional social and legal restrictions upon their own group.   Women in office may not
consider themselves as representative of any female constituency; however, their isolated and unique status makes
them highly visible and subjects them to direct and indirect
pressures from various women's organizations.   Women
judges who do recognize a female constituency may limit
it to peers in the legal profession or broaden it to include
females of all ages and conditions with legal problems.
Their personal norms and attitudes toward sex roles in society would influence the direction of their decisions for
their constituencies.

Decisions affected by personal views are made within
a particular institutional structure.   The structural condition of tokenism may affect attitudes and decisions through
the special expectations and treatment of the token by the
dominant members.   Tokens, according to Kanter, "are
people identified by ascribed characteristics ... that carry
with them a set of assumptions about culture, status, and
behavior highly salient for majority category members." [8]
The dominants, in this case male judges, may act to emphasize rather than reduce the differences defined in the
sex-role stereotypes.   Lawyers and judges who are women
resent the nomenclature of "women lawyers" and "women
judges," since they disagree with the social tradition that
gender is a salient characteristic in professional work.
The term "woman judge" is used in this study only because
of its convenience for the analysis of key variables.   (A
matching sample of male judges is being surveyed, and a
comparative analysis will be forthcoming.)

The woman in public office who does not define and
respond to a constituency of professional women or of mass
women, but instead emphasizes her personal interests in
career success, may be reacting to the realities of structural pressure.   Kanter[9] reports that in business token women
are expected to display loyalty to the male-dominated organization by ignoring or participating in prejudicial acts
toward members of their own gender.   She suggests that
the "queen-bee" syndrome, in which the token woman cred-
its her own inclusion to unique qualification and denigrates

the potential of other women, is not a role chosen by particular personalities but a natural response to the strains of minority status.

In this study the personal commitment of the women judges to feminism and the structural position of the women as tokens will be compared as explanations for various expectations, cognitions, attitudes, and decision-making propensities on women's issues.

Universe of Women Judges

During 1977 there were one hundred twenty-seven women sitting on general-jurisdiction courts in the forty-nine-state court system covered by this study. The four additional women serving in New Jersey in 1977 are not covered because of the state Supreme Court rule against surveys. Six women on the comparable court in the District of Columbia (Superior Court) were interviewed but not included in the mailed survey. The response rate to the questionnaire mailed during the winter and spring of 1978 was 65.4 percent, or eighty-three respondents of the universe of 127. This return is excellent for an elite operating in court cultures, which emphasize independence and separation from politics. The American Judicature Society survey of general-jurisdiction judges ("Identifying and Measuring Judicial Performance in American Trial Courts," supported by RANN) generated returns in fall 1977, just prior to this survey, of 63.2 percent. Their returns from women judges were at a lower rate than their overall average.

A comparison of the characteristics that are known about the universe to those of the respondents indicates a representative sample. Table 1 shows the similarities in background, age, place of birth, race, party, prior job experiences, years of private practice, and years of judicial experience. The only two descriptive elements that are somewhat less congruent are location by region and domestic status.

A smaller proportion of the universe in the East and South responded than in the Midwest and West. This difference, however, is not due to the culture of the South, which often appears in political studies. The few women judges in traditional Southern states responded with some enthusiasm to the opportunity to communicate about their special status

Table 1

Women Judges on Trial Courts, 1977:
Basic Characteristics

	Universe (127)		Sample (83)	
AGE:				
31-40	12	(9. 6%)	8	(9. 6%)
41-50	37	(29. 6%)	28	(33. 6%)
51-60	50	(40. 0%)	31	(37. 2%)
61-76	21	(16. 8%)	16	(19. 2%)
unk	7	(5. 6%)		
PLACE OF BIRTH				
same city	43	(33. 9%)	30	(36. 1%)
same state	29	(22. 8%)	20	(24. 1%)
same region	21	(16. 6%)	13	(15. 6%)
out-region	22	(17. 3%)	17	(20. 5%)
foreign	4	(3. 1%)	3	(3. 6%)
RACE: Black	10	(7. 9%)	6	(7. 2%)
PARTY:				
Democratic	92	(72. 4%)	62	(74. 7%)
Republican	27	(21. 3%)	19	(22. 9%)
PRIOR LAW JOBS:				
law faculty	11	(8. 7%)	7	(8. 4%)
prosecutor	33	(26. 0%)	21	(25. 3%)
state A-G	16	(12. 6%)	10	(12. 0%)
minor judge	56	(44. 1%)	35	(42. 2%)
federal job	11	(8. 7%)	7	(8. 4%)
YEARS PRIVATE PRACTICE:				
none	15	(12. 0%)	11	(13. 3%)
1-9	35	(27. 5%)	26	(31. 2%)
10-19	40	(30. 4%)	26	(31. 2%)
20 up	30	(23. 8%)	20	(24. 0%)
YEARS ON BENCH				
1-5	57	(45. 6%)	40	(48. 1%)
6-10	26	(20. 8%)	19	(22. 8%)
11-20	30	(24. 0%)	22	(26. 5%)
21 up	7	(5. 6%)	2	(2. 4%)

	Universe (127)		Sample (83)	
DOMESTIC STATUS:				
Ever married	101	(79.5%)	71	(85.5%)
No children	40	(32.0%)	23	(27.7%)
1-2 children	44	(35.2%)	32	(38.4%)
3 or more	36	(28.8%)	28	(33.6%)
REGION:				
East	35	(27.6%)	20	(24.1%)
South	28	(22.0%)	15	(18.1%)
Midwest	32	(25.2%)	23	(27.7%)
West	32	(25.2%)	25	(30.1%)

in that region.   The nonrespondents who depressed the
South and East rate were in Miami and New York City.
The AJS study also had lower response rates from New
York (50 percent) and Florida (56 percent) than their average.   This lesser interest probably reflects the combination
of overburdened metropolitan caseloads and a political sense
of self-preservation, carried by elite lawyers on the migration route from New York to Florida.   The Midwestern and
Western judges are generally less fearful that their answers
would have any impact upon their own careers.   A number
of the women judges in the East who did not find time for
the written questionnaire had been interviewed earlier (two
in New York City and two in Philadelphia).   There was
nothing unusual about their career or attitudes; some no
doubt felt that one form of access was sufficient for research purposes.

The curious difference between the universe and the
sample is in the domestic situation.   Those women who
never married were less likely to respond than those who
had ever married.   Those with no children responded less
than those with more.   An explanation may be found in the
kinds of questions asked about the management of professional and home roles and particularly about the support offered by spouses.   Those public women who "gave up" the
normal female role in favor of concentration on their profession are slightly underrepresented.   However, as Table
2 shows, the proportion of younger women judges who have
married is considerably greater than of the older women.
The smaller response rate from the East and South is also
related to the larger proportion of unmarried women and

Table 2

Universe of Women General Jurisdiction Judges by
Region, Age, and Domesticity

AGE	REGION				DOMESTICITY	
	East	South	Midwest	West	Ever Married	3 or More Children
31-40	0	3	6	3	12 (100%)	3 (25%)
41-50	6	10	10	11	31 (83.3%)	13 (4.19%)
51-60	14	9	11	16	39 (78%)	15 (38.5%)
61-76	13(37.1%)	5(22%)	3(11.5%)	2(7.1%)	16 (76.2%)	6 (37.5%)
unk	2	1	2	0	3 (60%)	-------
DOMESTICITY						
Ever Married	25(71.4%)	22(78.6%)	26(81.3%)	28(87.5%)	101(79.5%)	37 (36.6%)
3 or More Children	8(32%)	6(27.2%)	11(42.3%)	12(42.9%)	37(36.6%)	-------

women with smaller families serving as judges there.   The
new generation of women judges increasingly combines marriage and career; so the response sample is probably pre-
dictive of future universes.

       The similarity in ascribed and socialization char-
acteristics indicates that the respondents probably also represent the universe in respect to feminism and women's issues.   The distribution of members of the two major parties
in the sample matches the universe, and a feminist commitment is significantly related to party affiliation.

       The women judges were asked to identify them-
selves as feminists or not, allowing them to provide their
own definitions.   The presumption is that "feminist" carries
connotations of the belief in equal merit of the sexes and an
active commitment to equal access to all social roles.   The
sample also fits the universe for the structural variable of
number of women sitting together; there is a woman without
a gender colleague on 39.8 percent of the sample and 40
percent of the universe; two women sitting together on 20.5
percent of the sample and 18.5 percent of the universe; and
three or more women together on 39.8 percent of the sample and 41.5 percent of the universe.

Law: Primus Intervariables

       The primary explanation for any judicial decision
within the American tradition of jurisprudence is "the law."
The particular rule that would nullify policies to provide opportunities for new roles for women (and excluded minorities) is the interpretation of the Fourteenth Amendment equal-
protection clause as prohibiting "reverse discrimination."

       The Supreme Court faced the reverse discrimina-
tion issue in Bakke (1978), deciding that the distribution of
public goods on the crude basis of ascriptive identification
by suspect class is not constitutional.   The Court has refused to declare sex a suspect classification; so that tech-
nically under the precedent of Muller (1908) programs to
undo discrimination against women face less difficult exercises in logic than those for racial and ethnic minorities.
The Supreme Court has not yet developed standards for
identifying legitimate programs that assign scarce goods,
such as education and employment, in more sophisticated
ways to those formerly denied access.

Trial judges can apply their own notion of the legality of affirmative-action programs within the large lacuna left by the Supreme Court at the end of the 1977 term. Judges who doubt the constitutionality of compensatory programs are unlikely to take advantage of opportunities in their own courtrooms to make redistributions to women. Those who expect the Court to legitimize most existing affirmative-action programs are likely to make decisions that fit that view of the law. The attitude of women judges toward the legitimacy of this public policy was probed with the following statement: "Affirmative action for women and minorities is a form of discrimination against the majority." Those who agree (34.8 percent) would be unlikely to violate their definition of the law to open doors for other women.

Women who doubt the legality of affirmative action are also unable to see the need for such programs. They explain discrimination in personal rather than structural terms. On the other hand, women who feel that affirmative action is constitutional do recognize the existence of unequal treatment of women in formerly male occupations, including the legal profession. Thus their views of what is legitimate and of what is needed fit; those who see more sex discrimination have a legally acceptable program; those who see less need for public support of "outsiders" do not accept the legality of affirmative-action-type policy.

Since the meaning of the equal-protection clause in this policy area is in flux until the Court provides more useful precedents, the choice of interpretation of a trial judge is no doubt influenced by salient attitudes. A majority of feminist judges (62.5 percent) see affirmative-action programs as legitimate, as do a minority of nonfeminist judges (46.3 percent). The difference is not significant, suggesting that their notions of the law have other bases besides personal preference. On the other hand, one would not expect to find the law defined differently according to the degree of tokenism experienced by the judge herself. In fact, the percentage of judges who accept the legality of affirmative action is substantially the same whether the woman sits with or without a same-sex colleague, 52.9 percent and 54.2 percent, respectively.

Individual-Level Variables: Feminism

Judges' attitudes are closely related to their decisions, particularly in areas of discretion over developing public policy.[10] If a judge recognizes the existence of sex discrimination and feels a commitment toward full equality for women, then her cognitions and values are likely to suit her courtroon behavior.

A majority of women judges perceive that women want a social role outside of the home but face institutional resistance. They agree by a large majority (73.5 percent) that it is "right" for women to move into positions now dominated by males. In regard to their own entrance into a male-dominated institution, they feel highly visible, noticed, and criticized more than male judges. They recognize higher barriers to the achievement of nonprofessional women than to their own careers.

A consensual majority (89.1 percent) purport to be "basically sympathetic to the goals of the women's movement." However, sympathy is weaker than commitment to change. To tap the strength of their dedication to full sex equality, they were asked whether they considered themselves to be "feminists." Almost half (49.4 percent) identify themselves under this rubric. Admitting to being a feminist is a brave posture for a woman judge. The public is ambivalent about participation of women in some social organizations and anxious about the implications of equal status for important institutions like family and church. The communities most relevant to women judges, the legal profession and the courts, have a long tradition of sex discrimination in their internal affairs. A diffuse women's-rights movement and weak women's organizations without strong connections to political and legal organizations do not provide much support for women judges who are openly feminist.

As might be expected, those who consider themselves feminists are also liberal in their political philosophy. If one aspect of liberalism is openness to change and to democratization of political participation, then those who approve new roles for women in social institutions from which they have been excluded would fit the liberal frame. Of the liberal judges, 76.7 percent were feminists; of the moderates 38.5 percent; and of the conservatives 16.7 percent. The difference is significant. Since most women judges belong to the Democratic Party, Democrats are in the majority of both the feminist and nonfeminist categories. The relationship between Democratic partisanship and fem-

inism is significant, but less so than the relationship of
liberalism and feminism.

Feminism and Related Cognitions and Attitudes

Feminists are more likely to expect to have some
opportunity for service to women's rights from the bench
than are nonfeminists.   The difference is not quite significant, probably because judges on state trial courts know
as a matter of fact that federal judges have broader jurisdiction over sex discrimination matters.   Feminists also
consider sex-discrimination cases more important than nonfeminists do, in comparison to other kinds of cases on their
dockets.

Feminists understand the limitations upon women's
roles in terms of structure rather than sex characteristics.
A significantly large number of feminist judges (89.5 percent) agree that absence of "women in leadership positions
is mostly due to lack of opportunity and encouragement."
Attitudes as well as cognitions about woman's place separate
the feminists from the nonfeminists.   Feminists reveal a
strong consensus (80.5 percent) on allowing women into com-
bat forces; less than half of the nonfeminists approve the
removal of statutory restrictions on female participation.
The difference in attitude toward women taking on a responsibility that involves entirely "unfeminine" abilities is very
significant.

One symbol of female liberation from subservient
status in marriage, the rejection of the husband's last name,
produces quite different reactions from feminist and nonfeminist judges.   The use of a different name is considered
reasonable by 88 percent of the feminists and is disapproved
by a majority of nonfeminists.   The desire to preserve the
symbol of oneness in marriage reflects a conservative commitment to traditional domestic roles for both sexes.   Approval of relaxation of the tradition indicates feminist acceptance of evolutionary change in domestic relationships.
Loss of traditional symbols is the last and perhaps most
powerful indicator of structural and normative change in an
institution.

Feminism and Decision Making

The relationship of feminism to behavior was

examined by presenting the respondents with simulated cases involving typical sex-role changes demanded by ordinary
women.   The case conflicts involve both ends and means,
the wisdom of the change in women's place and the costs of
the policy to organizations and members of society.   One
case involves changing roles at the expense of a local public agency, a school board.   Another involves symbol change
at the psychic expense of a private party but with implications for the marital relationship for society as a whole.
The third case involves more autonomy in life choice for
women at the price of weakening the power of traditional
institutions (church, state) and of husbands.

The three cases as presented to the respondents
and the percentage indicating a propensity toward a feminist decision follow:

1.   The parents of a fifth-grade girl file suit against
     her school for refusing to allow her to play soc-
     cer on the school team.   The boy's team is the
     only one for her age group in town.   The coach
     and the boys are opposed.   Would you order the
     school to let her play?   Yes **65.1 percent**

2.   A married woman with two children files a peti-
     tion to change her last name to her maiden name.
     Her husband disapproves and argues that it will
     be embarrassing to him and their two school-age
     children.   Would you approve the name change?
     Yes **62.7 percent**

3.   A husband is separated from his wife and wants a
     temporary injunction to stop her from having an
     abortion during her second month of pregnancy.
     He does not want the child himself but promises
     to pay child support if she will raise the child.
     Would you give him the writ to stop the abortion?
     No **74.7 percent**

In the soccer case a much larger majority of feminists (75.6 percent) than nonfeminists would decide for the
female student.   The difference was not significant.   Still
it was wide enough to raise questions about the application
of precedent by the conservative judges.   The statutory law
is clearer in respect to equal treatment by educational institutions than the constitutional law in respect of affirmative-action programs.

Feminist and nonfeminist judges disagree significantly in the name case.   The feminists support symbolic change at about the same level as behavioral change (78 percent), but only a minority of nonfeminist judges would allow the woman to succeed in her case (46.3 percent).   The nonfeminist attitude and simulated behavior are congruent.

The abortion case raises sensitive issues affecting traditional national standards of morality and intermeshed social institutions.   The majorities of both feminists and nonfeminists would decide for the woman 80.5 percent and 63.3 percent, respectively.   Agreement here probably reflects the power of clear precedent over attitude.   The different support levels of the woman's choice by the judges in the two categories is not significant.

The feminists are quite consistent in their putative responses to women's demands upon the courts.   The clearest national precedent produces the largest majority; and the issue involving a minor where regional or local precedents may apply receive a lesser majority.   But the responses are within five percentage points.   The range of putative decisions of nonfeminists is over twenty percentage points.   Their highest support fits the Supreme Court abortion precedents; their strongest disapproval goes to the symbolic change.

Feminism and the Judicial Role

Just as women judges see the problems of ordinary women in terms of structural barriers, they recognize similar restraints upon the careers of women in the legal profession.   Feminists think that their abilities are not given full scope in the male-dominated court systems.   Sixty-two percent of the feminists but only 29 percent of the nonfeminists agree that "female judges have to be twice as good as male judges to get the same recognition for competence." The feminists disagree more with the nonfeminists over their own status than over the condition of nonprofessionals. Feminists are also more likely to feel visible on the basis of sex and to experience prejudice from male judges and attorneys.

Women judges probably interpret their treatment by the numerically dominant male judges in court according to their ideological expectations.   Almost half of the feminists

(44. 4 percent) report that male judges treat them in coldly formal fashion.   However, a significantly smaller proportion of nonfeminists (15 percent) report this experience.   A bare majority of nonfeminists think that they are treated as 100-percent equal colleagues by males on the bench; only a minority of feminists feel such complete acceptance.

The important issues to women lawyers concern the various access points to the profession, i. e. , admissions to law school, clerkships, partnerships in legal firms, and policy-level law jobs in government.   Strong feminists might be expected to approve affirmative-action-type policies for access to legal as well as other social institutions.

Judges have more discretion in selecting law clerks (where the court budgets this kind of support) than in deciding cases.   Each woman judge was asked, on the assumption that she could choose a law clerk, whether she would prefer women or men or be sex-neutral in choosing among applicants.   The large majority of judges (78. 3 percent) take the legally sound position of sex neutrality in their own employment practices.   Only ten, evidently trying to redress past discrimination against young women law-school graduates, would give preference to women.   Twenty-two percent of the feminists would prefer women; and only 2. 4 percent of nonfeminists.   Three (all nonfeminists) would prefer men.   In this instance neutrality is unlikely to serve as a shield for sex bias, since the women can depend upon themselves to treat women candidates without sex bias.

Judges have authority to decide cases and choose law clerks, but they cannot select other judges (with a few exceptions, such as the election of Associate Judges by the Circuit Judges in Illinois).   In order to discover how they feel about the token number of women lawyers on the bench, respondents were asked for their normative position on the composition of the U. S. Supreme Court.   An affirmative-action answer would be that one Justice of the nine should be female, since the contemporary pool of female eligibles is proportional to one seat.   In fact, only 22. 9 percent of the respondents gave the affirmative-action answer.   A minority (25. 3 percent) would take a sex-neutral stance and refuse to recommend that sex should be a major criterion for even one seat.   A majority of the women judges proposed more than one woman Justice, which suggests that they think merit-based selection would produce more than one woman Justice.

Although Presidents from Franklin Roosevelt through Ford have considered women candidates, all of the 101 Justices to date have been male. The lack of even token representation may have spurred the generous norms of the women judges. Moreover, their sex-neutral standard for clerks stands in sharp contrast to the specification of goals for the Supreme Court. They probably trust their own objectivity in evaluation of qualifications more than the objectivity of the President, Senate, and ABA.

Feminists recommend a goal larger than proportional to the pool; 53.9 percent prefer two or more women on the Court. A significantly smaller proportion of nonfeminists (29.3 percent) indicate such high expectations. However, there is a consensus among the women judges that at least one Justice would be right. The presence of a woman Justice would be symbolic of the integration of women into legal political institutions. To nonfeminists she would mean opportunity for women lawyers, and to feminists she would also mean hope for new rules for all women.

System-Level Variables: Tokenism

The structural model of behavior developed by Kanter[11] offers a second broad explanation for behavior of women judges. This model asserts that opportunity structure, power structure, and proportional membership in the organization mold the behavior of members of work groups more than personal qualities. Since research on women judges concerns women who have already achieved prestigious positions, the variables of opportunity structure and power structure are less useful than proportionality. Yet women judges are in a distinct minority in their court organizations. Thus the variable of proportional membership remains useful in examining the impact of structure.

Token members of a group may act differently and be treated differently from members of large minorities or potential majorities. The high visibility of tokens bring them more attention than may be utilitarian for achievement or satisfaction in their work. They are seen by the dominant members through the filter of generalized stereotypes. The smaller the proportion of women in a court, the more visible gender becomes to others and the less likely is the token's inclination to adopt attitudes or play roles that would increase the salience of that characteristic. Admitting to feminist convictions and reaching out to identify women's issues emphasizes gender identity. A woman judge in a token situation may feel a tension between her short-term personal interest in casting off the stigma of gender, even by assimilating with the majority view of woman's place, and her long-term interest in improving the status of the class.

Kanter measures the proportionality variable by the size of the subgroup. [12] Skewed groups include 20 percent or fewer outsiders or tokens; tilted groups include 21-40 percent outsiders or minorities; and balanced groups contain "ins" and "outs" of 41-60 percent of the membership. Whether these cutting points will be the most useful to distinguish problems associated with the integration of previously excluded class members can only be verified by empirical studies.

On the major trial courts in metropolitan areas (over 250,000 population), women in no instance make up over 20 percent of the judiciary; in terms of Kanter's taxonomy, they are all tokens. Of the eighty-three respondents in this study twelve women sitting without a female colleague on small courts constitute by themselves more than 20 percent of their benches, half on tilted and half on balanced courts. The Kanter categories are obviously more useful in large organizations, since 25 percent representation on a four-judge court means something different from 25 percent on a hundred-judge court. In fact, the "small group" may be oppressive in demanding conformity of an outsider member who constitutes a fourth of the whole, while a large group might be able to tolerate and ignore (not encourage or share with) outsiders who only constitute 5 percent. In view of these considerations, since the size of the courts range from one to 181 (in Los Angeles), the proportionality variable will not be measured by percentage but by raw number of women. Of the eighty-three respondents, thirty-four (40.9 percent) sit without a woman colleague; the other forty-nine, with one or more other women. Those sitting with no female peer are denominated tokens.

Another measure of proportionality on the court is the newness of women as outsiders. Just under half of the women are the first of their sex on their benches (44.6 percent). About a third (31.4 percent) are the second or third women ever to have served on that court; and the remaining twenty judges are fourth or higher. Thus 76 percent of the 1977 women judges are working in organizations with little or no experience with sex integration.

Women in groups produce more feminists (58.3 percent) than women tokens (38.2 percent), although the difference is not quite significant. Unconventional attitudes are easier for judges to sustain with some peer support. Expectations for opportunities to deal with women's-rights cases varies significantly by proportionality. Of those sitting as tokens, only 9.7 percent foresaw the possibility of service to other women through case decisions. Almost a third of the women with one or more female peers have higher expectations for sex discrimination cases on their dockets.

Cognitions of structural barriers to women's growth and development do not differ by degree of tokenism. Attitudes toward assumption of male roles by women were the same for women alone and women in small groups. However, there was a tendency for women with same-sex peers to approve symbolic change more than women tokens. In making simulated decisions in the soccer, name, and abortion cases, no difference could be attributed to structural situation.

Tokenism and Judicial Role

Women judges with same-sex colleagues perceive the attitude of their male colleagues as apprehensive and requiring that they prove themselves. Women judges who have had predecessors report that the male judges are condescending but do not require proof of ability. The male judges seem more welcoming to women who are single tokens and are the first of their kind than they do to women with colleagues or predecessors. A large majority of the women judges (80.7 percent) feel that the male judges welcome their presence. However, sizable minorities report that some male judges are noncommittal toward their presence (27.7 percent) or formal and distant toward them (26.5 percent). Some (16.9 percent) report being ignored. Others note that male judges act uncomfortable (15.7 percent) or resentful (10.8 percent) toward their joining the exclusive group. The emotional ambience may be a different matter from, although affecting, the work relationships. Formality is appropriate among colleagues in a public organization and certainly more utilitarian than hostility. Trial judges even

on multijudge benches enjoy a great deal of autonomy, controlling their own courtroom business without supervision,
except in the largest courts with administrative judges.
Their de jure powers are equal; so that reactions to women
as colleagues must be based on their personal rather than
organizational resources.   Women who serve in token status
feel more formality than those with at least one "sister" on
the bench; but half of the judges in both groups have a sense
of high visibility on the basis of sex to male judges and
lawyers.

The judges' cognitions of discrimination in the courts
do not relate significantly to their own structural situations.
Women with two or more female colleagues agree (42.9 percent) that the system requires them to be twice as good as
males to succeed.   A similar minority of those alone (38.2
percent) report such pressure.   The small difference does
not fit the hypothesis that token women would be more hes-
itant in recognizing or admitting unfair treatment toward
themselves.   Since a substantial minority of both categories
feel institutionally constrained, consciousness of biased
treatment does not require an exchange of experiences with
another woman on the same bench.   The reference group
that provides support for these judges may be women in
the legal profession rather than women judges.

In general, women on the bench know very little
about the personalities, experiences, or attitudes of women
judges in other jurisdictions, even within the same state.
Their cognitions and beliefs depend upon their own immediate
experience.   Evidently the structural condition of the token
is not different enough from that of women with a few colleagues to produce any variety of cognitions and beliefs.

Token women judges report higher norms for the
representation of women on the Supreme Court than those
with peers.   Almost a third of the tokens (32.4 percent)
recommend more women Justices than would be proportional to the national pool of women lawyers.   The token may
understand better than the other women judges the costs of
her position and not wish to place a woman on the Supreme
Court in the same structural situation.   The choice of high
goals rather than realistic goals for women on the Court also indicates a strong vote of support for the competency of
female candidates.

Summary

Feminism is useful in distinguishing the cognitions, attitudes, and decisional directions of women judges, but feminism only distinguishes between greater and lesser positive support for the liberation of ordinary women from traditional roles. Nonfeminists are somewhat less likely to recognize the barriers and propose radical solutions to their own problems as women judges in a male institution. But the important finding is that women judges are conscious of institutional constraints and more favorable toward new social roles for women who demand them than the general female population.[13] Even the nonfeminists are ahead of public opinion on women's liberation.

Proportionality is somewhat less useful in understanding differences in women judges' views on sex integration. However, there may not be enough variation in tokenism in 1977 to provide an appropriate test of its explanatory value. When women judges constitute over 20 percent in some large metropolitan courts, it may be possible to devise a rigorous test of the impact of structure upon attitude and behavior.

Moreover, the personal variables no doubt interact with structural variables in such complex ways that sorting out the direction and strength of relationship would not be an easy task. Structures exist in environmental contexts, and governmental organizations are subject to the pressures of changing opinion and cultural norms. Even tokenism might be overcome by environmental support. A strong woman's movement or well-organized women lawyers in a judicial district might offset structural limitations upon judicial roles. In 1977, however, women judges give strong approval to sex equality despite skewed structures and traditional environments.

Notes

[1]Judith Long Laws, "The Psychology of Tokenism: An Analysis," Sex Roles 1 (1975): 51-67; Joyce Jennings Walstedt, "Women as Marginals," Psychological Report 34 (1974): 639-646.

[2]Susan Tolchin, "The Exclusion of Women from the Judicial Process," Signs: Journal of Women in Culture and Society 2 (1977): 877-887.

3Jeane Kirkpatrick, The New Presidential Elite (New York: Russell Sage Foundation and the Twentieth Century Fund, 1976).

4Susan Welch, "Women as Political Animals? A Test of Some Explanations for Male-Female Political Participation Differences," American Journal of Political Science 21 (1977): 711-730.

5Irene Diamond, Sex Roles in the State House (New Haven: Yale University Press, 1977).

6Sharyne Merritt, "Winners and Losers: Sex Differences in Municipal Elections," American Journal of Political Science 21 (November 1977): 731-743; Nikki R. Van Hightower, "The Recruitment of Women for Political Office," American Politics Quarterly (July 1977): 301-314; Marcia M. Lee, "Why Few Women Hold Public Office," Political Science Quarterly 91 (Summer 1976): 297-314.

7But see Marianne Githens, "Spectators, Agitators, or Lawmakers: Women in State Legislators," in Marianne Githens and Jewel L. Prestage, eds., A Portrait of Marginality (New York: David McKay, 1977); Herbert M. Kritzer and Thomas M. Uhlman, "Sisterhood in the Courtroom: Sex of Judge and Defendant in Criminal Case Disposition," Social Science Journal 14 (1977): 77-88.

8Rosabeth Moss Kanter, "Some Effects of Proportions on Group Life: Skewed Sex Ratios and Response to Token Women," American Journal of Sociology 82 (1976): 968.

9Ibid., p. 979.

10Glendon Schubert, The Judicial Mind Revisited (New York: Oxford University Press, 1974).

11Rosabeth Moss Kanter, Men and Women of the Corporation (New York: Basic Books, 1977).

12Ibid., p. 209.

13Virginia Slims American Women's Opinion Poll, Vol. III, 1974. Roper Organization.

ORGANIZATIONAL ROLE ORIENTATIONS
ON FEMALE-DOMINANT COMMISSIONS:
FOCUS ON STAFF-COMMISSIONER INTERACTION

Debra W. Stewart

Historically, women's organizational involvement has been
in predominantly female organizations. The locus of activity has varied--the church, the female auxiliary to a male
professional group, or at times the community itself. The
focus, however, has been on issues around which women as
a group could mobilize concern and effort. By now we have
developed a fairly rich literature exploring the structure of
these organizations, with the League of Women Voters perhaps receiving the greatest attention. Still, relatively little
is known about the organizational roles women play in predominantly female public or private organizations, and virtually nothing is known about the relationship between board
and staff within such groups.

        This article reports on a significant female-dominated
public organization, the local Commission on the Status of
Women. Within that organization the respective roles played
by commission members and staff serve as the particular
focal point. Staff-commissioner roles in CSW merit investigation on both theoretical and practical grounds.

The introduction of a staff to any organization suggests a new element potentially capable of shaping the decision-making process of that unit. If the organization is a government board or commission to which persons have been elected or appointed because they are presumed to represent some definable constituency in the community, the introduction of a staff may function either positively or negatively toward that end. Staff may bring more efficient and effective implementation of board will; alternatively, or perhaps simultaneously, it may mean the emergence of a new, nonpolitically responsible force mediating board will. Though in theory there is a clear division between commissioner and staff roles, the literature strongly suggests a very clouded reality.

The bulk of this literature focuses on policy-making boards and suggests that full-time staff strongly influence board decisions.[1] Scholars reporting this finding attribute staff influence to a combination of greater staff knowledge and time. In varying degrees this empirically based literature addresses the normative question posed by staff dominance. Yet concern with the normative question may be premature. Some recent analyses suggest a more varied and less inevitable set of commissioner-staff relationships may prevail on some kinds of citizen boards. Wilson's synthesis of the literature on board-staff relationships in voluntary organizations concludes: "When holding lay office in a voluntary association is in itself a source of substantial rewards to the incumbent, the influence of the appointed staff is likely to be lessened and that of board members heightened."[2] And at least one recent study of government commissions suggests that the "domination (by staff) is considerably less than much of the literature would lead us to believe."[3]

This paper originates in two beliefs: first, that staff dominance on Commissions on the Status of Women is not an inevitable outcome of staff assignment to a board; second, that where staff dominance occurs its ill effects cannot be assumed automatically.

The first part of the paper describes Commissions on the Status of Women as organizations and then elaborates the data base for this study. Next, three sets of questions, linked to the theoretical and practical concerns articulated above, are explored. First, how do commissioners and staff view their respective roles, and what types of role relationships emerge from these sets of orientations? Second, how do board characteristics relate to role relationships? Third, what is the actual value congruence between commissioners and staff, and how well does value congruence predict role orientation of commissioners toward staff?

Commissions on the Status of Women

Commissions on the Status of Women merit attention because they reflect a large-scale, government-endorsed effort to institutionalize female participation in community-level decision making across the United States. This institutionalization effort dates from the 1963 report of the President's Commission on the Status of Women entitled American Women. Spurred on by recommendations of that report, the Women's Bureau (U. S. Department of Labor) spearheaded the mobilization of groups throughout the fifty states behind the idea of state-level advisory Commissions on the Status of Women. With Women's Bureau encouragement many states fostered the establishment of local commissions charged with similar tasks. Currently there are active CSW in over 150 local jurisdictions throughout the United States. While these commissions vary greatly in terms of structure, resources, relationship to local government, self-definition, etc., they have a common raison d'être of providing a forum for consideration of the status of women in local communities.

Typically the local impetus for establishing a commission comes from women occupying leadership roles in women's organizations within the community. While the amount of preplanning and number of individuals involved varies, all commissions share a common birth experience in their official enactment by a local policy-making institution. The two broad types of enactment documents are executive orders and local ordinances. Executive orders, constituting the authorization for some local commissions, offer the advantage of greater freedom for commissions in defining programs and procedures. Typically, however, commission advocates prefer establishment by ordinance, which provides greater promise of continuity and possibly greater resources. In either case the enactment document generally spells out many of the organizational details, including size and appointment of membership, reporting procedures and staffing arrangements.

Commissions vary in size, ranging, according to a

1975 Women's Bureau survey, 4 from seven to forty members, with the mayor typically making the appointments when the authorization is by executive order and a variety of appointment arrangements holding for statutory commissions. As a rule, these statutory commissions, established by ordinance, follow the local government's standard procedure for appointments to citizen commissions. It may mean that the mayor, or chief executive officer, appoints and the city or county council approve appointments; it may require each councilmember to make a certain number of appointments--the practices vary. Citizen commissioners are not monetarily compensated for service.

The location of the commission in the local government establishes the line of accountability. Some commissions (29.2 percent) report directly to the mayor or chief executive officer of the jurisdiction; others (43.8 percent) report directly to the legislative body (county board, city council, county commission); still others (16.7 percent) report to an administrative official, such as a Director of the Human Relations Commission, who in turn reports to the next higher administrative official.

Commissions on the Status of Women generally enjoy substantial discretion in organizing the internal operations. Some commissions operate with executive committees; some do not. Most commissions establish both standing and ad hoc committees to accomplish their objectives. Some commissions allow noncommission members to serve on commission committees; others do not. In the absence of a formal requirement that the commission chair be appointed by a specific official, commissions tend to elect their chairs by a simple majority vote. The budget picture for commissions also varies. While a full 61 percent of the commissions responding to a Women's Bureau survey reported no budget in FY 1975-1976, those funded commissions reported levels varying from $75 to $79,000.

Currently many local commissions are unstaffed or staffed only minimally. Just under a third of the commissions (31.3 percent) surveyed in 1975 reported employing executive directors; only 18.3 percent reported additional nonclerical staff beyond a single executive director. What does appear to be a consistent theme across most commissions surveyed in 1975 is a common desire for and pressure in the direction of increased staff support.

Data Base

This study focuses on commissioner-staff relationships on five successful CSW.   Since the objective of this
paper is to illuminate the range of possibilities for commission-staff relations in well-working systems, it was
necessary to select CSW that were perceived as successful.

The five commissions studied were selected because
they were viewed as "effective" or successful commissions
by a panel of seven women, all of whom have held positions
in organizations where they have been directly concerned
with the establishment and promotion of local CSW.   Each
member of the panel was asked, in a telephone interview,
a series of questions designed to elicit, first, her impres-
sions of the meaning of effectiveness when applied to Commissions on the Status of Women, and second, her nominations of commissions placing in the top five or six according to this definition.   While there was some variation in
those commission attributes named as signifying effectiveness, there was surprising consensus on which commissions
fell into the most effective or successful group.   One of
those commissions was dropped from the analysis because
of its unique government setting.[5]   The panel consensus
was supported as well by the survey data, which indicated
high activity levels for these commissions, though the level
of staff support varied across the five communities.

Studying these commissions involved visiting the
communities for a period of from six to nine days.   In
every community I conducted interviews with commission
leadership and staff.   The commission members interviewed
included the executive officers of the commission, plus the
chairpersons of all active task forces or committees.   These
interviews generally lasted from ninty minutes to two hours.
The interviews with the commission executive director and/
or other staff were much more lengthy.   The total time
spent interviewing staff ranged from two and one-half hours,
in one commission with only part-time staff support, to
seven hours in the more heavily staffed commissions.   From
six to ten commission members and staff were interviewed
in each community.

The interview schedule employed included open-ended
questions probing commissioner and staff perception of their
own and each others' roles.   As well, forced-choice questions

asked commissioners and staff to assign value priorities to
commission activities and concerns.   Two kinds of activities
and concerns were considered.   The list of goal activity
areas to which commissioners and staff were asked to respond was constructed from a review of 1975 Women's Bureau survey of local CSW coupled with information generated
in a pilot study of one local commission in North Carolina.
The list of substantive policy issues was drawn primarily
from the national women's agenda.[6]   The eleven items and
seventy-five subitems appearing on that agenda were melded
into a list of twenty substantive issues and put in terms
commonly identifiable across communities studied.   Commissioners and staff ranked each activity area and issue
concern on a five-point importance scale.

Additionally, a mailed questionnaire yielded personal-
profile information on each commissioner and staff member,
including both demographic data and data on extra CSW organizational activity levels of commissioners and staff.

Commissioners and Their Staff:
Role Orientations in Five Communities

One conclusion often drawn from a finding of staff
dominance over board members is that its occurrence is
an inevitable counterpart of efficiency and effectiveness--
hallmarks of a successful organization.   Still, it is not
obvious that staff dominance is a prerequisite of success
for citizen's advisory commissions.   Especially where the
citizen board is created to facilitate increased citizen input,
the necessary association of staff dominance with success
is suspect.

Exploration of the role relationships in the five successful Commissions on the Status of Women, selected as
described above, permits assessment of the "necessary"
character of staff dominance for these institutions.   A brief
discussion of the role concept and a presentation of a con-
struct for classifying sets of role orientations, provide a
framework for description of the five commissions studied
here.

The term "role," as used in this study, corresponds
to that notion employed by Wahlke et al. in their analysis
of legislative roles.   "Role" there suggests a coherent set
of "norms" of behaviors that are thought by those involved

in the interactions being viewed to apply to all incumbents
of a position. [7] In the Wahlke study expressed norms and
behavior are viewed as closely related: "The concept postu-
lates that individual legislators are aware of the norms constituting the role and consciously adapt their behavior to
them in some fashion."[8] So also in this analysis of local
commissioners and staff the assumption is that norms constituting the role inform behavior. Thus information on the
role relationships between commissioners and staff gives insight into the behaviors that are likely to follow from incumbency in one of those roles.

       To characterize the commissioner-staff roles in these
five commissions, we have considered the content of the
role orientations for each group. The role orientations of
each are visualized along two axes, representing the dimensions of commissioner behavior expected from self and staff,
and staff behavior expected from self and commissioners,
in each case extending from deferring to controlling behavior. [9] In other words, the commissioners can define their
roles in terms of the extent to which they control the decision-making process or defer to the staff in that process;
as well, staff can place themselves on the same continuum
in terms of the extent to which they defer to commissioners
or attempt to control the decision-making process.

       In this study I asked the principal staff member and
the commission leadership (executive committee, officers,
heads of major committees) to answer the question: "In
terms of initiating activities and deciding how to pursue
them, do you believe that decision making should be in the
hands of the commission, the staff, or shared equally by
the commission and staff?"

       If a commissioner answered, "In the hands of the
commission," she was classified as "controlling" in role
orientation. If she responded, "In the hands of the staff,"
she was classified as "deferring" in role orientation. If
she responded, "In the hands of both," she was classified
as "sharing" in role orientation. The staff defined itself
in terms of the same continuum.

       The range of possible types of commissioner-staff
role orientation and the actual location of commissions studied is reflected in Figure 1. To protect the anonymity of
commissions and respondents, fictitious names are given to
the five commissions studied.

The vertical axes reflect the commissioner perspective.   Position for commissioners was determined by
the mean response of the commissioner group.   The staff
response reflects simply the response of the principal staff
person.   The role set for the commission as a unit is defined by plotting these two positions for each commission.
Beside each commission named is the role orientation of
commissioners and their staff.   For example, in Onega the
role orientation of the commission leadership was unanimously controlling, while the staff held a sharing-control per-
spective--resulting in a (+1.0, 0.0) location on the grid in
Figure 1.   In St. George four of the six members of com-

Figure 1

Role Orientations of Commissioners and Staff on
Five Local Commissions on the Status of Women

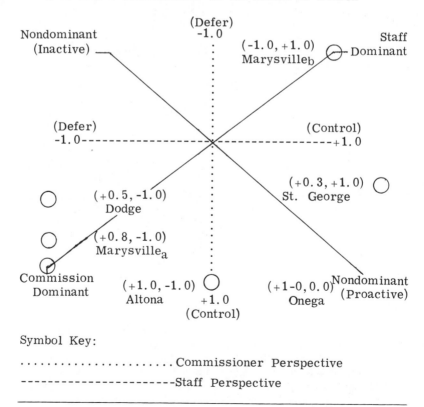

Symbol Key:

. . . . Commissioner Perspective

-----------------------Staff Perspective

mission leadership were sharing in perspective and two were
controlling, while the executive director was purely controlling in her orientation--resulting in a $(+.3, +1.0)$ location
on the grid.   One commission, Marysville, found it necessary to distinguish one functional area of staff activity from
the normal operations of the commission in order to answer
this question.   The result was two sets of role relationships
reflected on the grid for Marysville: Marysville a $(+.8, -1.0)$ and Marysville b $(-1.0, +1.0)$.

Each of the four quadrants of the grid are labeled by
the pure forms that they represent at the corner points.
The location $(-1.0, -1.0)$ represents the Nondominant, Inactive commission, where both commissioners and staff believe in deferring to the other.   The location $(-1.0, +1.0)$
is the pure Staff-Dominant Commission.   The opposite extreme is found in the Commission-Dominant quadrant, with
the $(+1.0, -1.0)$ location reflecting the pure form.   Finally,
the role orientations of commissioners and staff can be such
that both believe in controlling, as reflected in the Nondominant, Proactive type located at $(+1.0, +1.0)$ on the grid.

To understand more fully the meaning associated with
the actual locations on the grid assumed by each of these
five commissions studied, I asked commissioners and staff
to define the staff role on their commissions in relationship
to commissioners.   Answers provided by respondents aid in
assigning meaning to each set of role orientations found.

The commissioner-dominant commission fits the
classic model presented in the literature of public administration[10] with its taproot in the American reform tradition, envisioning citizen-commissioner sovereignty comple-
mented by value-neutral staff.   Two commissions, Altona
$(+1.0, -1.0)$ and Dodge $(+.5, -1.0)$, fits this model as reflected
by their placement in this quadrant.   One Dodge commission
member voiced the classic board-staff notion when she characterized the staff-commissioner relationship on her CSW
in this way:

> The staff work under us, at our request, to main-
> ly do the work of letter writing, filing, and cler-
> ical, and our director also will attend a lot of pub-
> lic hearings and meetings for us and then report
> ....   They perform sort of an information-gather-
> ing function to support the task forces and the
> leadership of the Commission.

This commissioner perspective fits well with the orientation of the executive director in Dodge, who characterized her role as carrying out the wishes of the advisory board.

> ... it is not my function to create issues for them or to bring issues to their attention, but to guide them, in a sense, as far as what's possible, what isn't possible ... and to carry out their wishes. And being as creative as a group as they are, they really don't need anyone else to bring ideas to them.

However, half of the commission leadership group in Dodge held as an ideal model one involving less directing and more sharing of initiative and direction with the executive director. One of these commissioners explained that she was slowly coming to rethink the commissioner-staff relationship in a way that leads to a recommendation for a more activist role for the staff.

> I'm changing my concept of what the role should be. I originally felt that the executive director should be a staff person, supportive of the policies established by the Commission. I'm now beginning to wonder whether or not a more innovative, active role on the part of the executive director may not be the way to go. Instead of her being merely a staff person, maybe she should be a professional leader of a commission. I haven't really come to a decision. I've always resented being a volunteer, appointed to a position and then being in a subservient position to a paid staff director. But in this very busy time, when people are becoming more and more professional, and volunteers rarely reach that total level of professionalism, I don't know that we shouldn't go the other way.... I'm ambivalent.

As the (+.5) location indicates, commission leadership was evenly split on their understanding of their own roles, with about half defining their role in terms of complete control, and half defining the control of the commission as most appropriately shared with the staff. Where discomfort arose in the commission-staff relationship here, it took the form of some commissioners wanting the executive director to be more active.

Altona also fell in the Commissioner-Dominant

quadrant; but it represents the pure case of totally congruent
role expectations.   Commission leadership unanimously supported total commission control; staff supported total deference to commissioners on commission business.   The staff
described its function as barely more than clerical:

> Administrative work--making sure the minutes are
> gotten out and that someone takes minutes of the
> meetings, that they are edited properly and mailed
> out in enough time for the commissioners to re-
> ceive before the next meeting ...

However, it is important to note that the Altona staff
is not full-time CSW staff.   The staff is loaned to the Commission by the Department of Human Resources.   Crucial
insight into the source of the superficially quiescent staff-
commissioner relationship emerges in the remarks of one
member of the CSW leadership.

> We don't really rely on the staff.   We have been
> led to believe that the staff is the staff of Human
> Resources, who are lent to us to do little things.
> And you feel rather guilty calling on them, be-
> cause it's like you're pulling them away from oth-
> er things.

In a third commission, Marysville, the role expectations of commissioners and staff emerged in two different
forms associated with two distinct charges of the commission.   In this case, the commission was entrusted with the
advisory responsibilities typical of all Commissions on the
Status of Women, but also was overseeing a women's center
operated by the CSW staff.   Figure 1 reflects this distinc-
tion with its two locations for the Marysville Commission
on the grid: Marysville a, referring to general CSW charge,
and Marysville b, referring to the women's-center activity.

With respect to the general CSW activity, the executive director saw her main role as liaison to local government and in general "to sort of see that everything that they
(commissioners) need done one way or another gets done."
On general CSW functioning, the commissioner perspective
tended to complement the executive director's view.   Typically commission leadership would explain: "The staff is
there ... to assist me in anything that I have to do, any-
time I need anything."   But one member of the leadership
group did not view the total commission control as good or

appropriate. Rather, she wanted to look to the executive director for some leadership even on general commission issues. In her ideal model this commissioner reported that the executive director "does two things. She facilitates implementation of things which were predecided, but she also seeds the ideas for new policies." Thus this commissioner was more desirous of greater sharing of control than was the executive director who, with respect to the general commission activities, was willing to defer.

Regarding the second charge of this commission, the women's center, the commissioners and staff perceptions of their roles were reversed but still complementary. The executive director's role as chief staff officer for the women's center was to supervise people and to run the center program. Commissioners did not want to be involved in controlling that program and were quite willing to give up all but the most tangential advisory function.

This manifestation of staff dominance in role orientation fits well the model described in the contemporary school-board literature predicting the inevitable dominance of staff over part-time citizen decision makers.[11] As far as the women's center was concerned both staff and commissioners recognized the staff's superior capacity for mobilizing information, negotiating with outside actors, etc., so commissioners were willing to follow the staff lead. However, it is worth noting that only one commission fell into this category of Staff Dominance, and it did so in terms of only one half of its charge.

Staff-commissioner role conflicts on the Marysville commission arose primarily from the commissioners' judgment that women's-center activity occupied too much staff time. Said one commissioner: "Now that we have the [women's center], the executive staff is going more towards running it as their function, and supporting the commission is almost a sideline."

The Nondominant, Proactive commission is characterized by a striving for control of decision making by both commissioners and staff. Clearly, the staff-commissioner role is blurred in this case, and room for conflict is great. As indicated in Figure 1, the St. George commission fits into this quadrant. Here the chief staff officer viewed her role as controlling the direction of the commission, while the commission leadership also held at least a moderately

controlling role definition. Reflecting the perspective that
staff should be in charge, the executive director described
her role to me in this way:

> I, in a sense, see myself as an initiator and a
> leader, and I have to play the game of it really
> coming from them. But in a sense, everybody
> knows the game we're playing. And the commis-
> sioners don't seem to resent that. . . . Occasion-
> ally I run into trouble when I want to do some-
> thing and when it gets to a commission meeting,
> it's tabled or it's not understood and you have to
> bring it back in a different form and so forth.
> But that has been the exception rather than the
> rule. My feeling very much is that the success
> of a commission really lies in the kind of leader-
> ship that the director brings to the commission,
> rather than the other way around.

Commissioner leadership on the St. George commission acknowledged the need for commissioners to defer to
staff in certain areas, but generally favored a shared control of commission direction. One commission leader explained this somewhat ambivalent position to me in this way.

> In my estimation, anyone that's going to be effec-
> tive as an executive director has to be someone
> who does not have to wait for someone else to
> give her directions. I think it's great that she
> can get input from the commission, that she can
> digest it, so to speak, and act according to the
> wishes of the commissioners; but also (that she
> can) be cognizant of the things that are going on...
> and bring information to the commission that they
> can use in making their decisions.

Still, at least two members of the six in the St.
George leadership group felt strongly that commissioners
should be the exclusive controlling force. "We make the
policy and she carries it out," was the way they described
their models. As one might expect, this commission had
a history of considerable commissioner-staff strife that
seemed, by 1977, to be reaching a resolution in favor of the
executive director.

In Onega the commissioner and staff perspectives of
their roles were just the reverse of that found in St. George.

Here, also, the propensity of both commissioners and staff
to define for themselves a controlling role had produced
substantial strife in the commission's history. But in the
Onega case, it seemed to be reaching a resolution that favored commissioners over staff.

Each commission leader described the role of the
chief staff person for the commission in roughly the same
way: "The executive director here is a coordinator who
works under volunteers, acting on their direction; and the
ruling body is clearly the commissioners' executive board."
In the commissioner view the controlling activity was defin-
itely not shared with the staff; but the executive staff office
had a rather different perspective. Seeing the staff role
as one of sharing the activity of directing the commission
with the commissioners, Onega's chief staff officer defined
her role in this way:

> The coordinator has to breathe life into volunteers
> constantly. . . . I think one of the biggest jobs of
> the coordinator is to constantly breathe life into
> volunteers and to make them want to participate
> and to extend energies to work. Frequently, if
> you are a volunteer with paid help, you fall into
> this pattern: "Well, what are they paid for?"
> . . . Technically, the coordinator does nothing but
> coordinate; in reality, [she] has to provide a cer-
> tain amount of leadership. A particular committee
> may be going off away from their goals or objec-
> tives, and it's up to you to very tactfully and nice-
> ly put them back toward their goals or objec-
> tives. . . .

None of the five successful commissions fits into the
Nondominant, Inactive type of commission--a model where
both commissioners and staff see themselves as deferring
to the others' lead. A commission may fall into this quadrant when all parties involved fear the cost of action of any
kind. It may occur where persons are appointed to the commission because they are perceived to be nonactivist and
where the staff is assigned to commission work in combination with a host of other duties. Clearly, the motivation
to control the decision-making process is likely to be low
for both parties in such cases. Such commissions are not
likely to be perceived as highly successful or highly effective commissions.[12] Thus we would not expect such commissions to appear in the subsample selected for intensive
study here.

The principal finding of this exploration into role orientations on five successful commissions is that staff dominance over board is not an inevitable correlate of success
for a Commission on the Status of Women. As noted above,
only one commission fell into the Staff-Dominant quadrant
and did so only in terms of one half of its charge.

If the relative propensity of commissioners and staff
to "control" or "defer" varies among successful commissions,
preference for a particular set of role orientations might
still prevail. But in order to bring preference to fruition,
understanding of the relationship between board characteristics and role orientations is crucial.

Commissioner Resources and Role Orientations

Any analysis of board-staff relationships should recognize that in such relationships each party brings to bear
certain resources. Zald[13] suggests resources may be classified as "detachable," those not closely tied to a person
and basically transferable; or "personal," relatively non-
transferable resources like sex or SES, and strategic contingency situations, or strategic decision points in a commission's life.[14] Board strength on some combination of
these factors can tip the balance of power in a board's direction. In this study of CSW "detachable resources" and
strategic contingency situations are considered in an effort
to illuminate the role relationships plotted above in Figure
1. Personal characteristics, defined by Zald as relatively
nondetachable resources, such as sex and SES, are not considered in this analysis. Variation on sex across commissions studied is minimal. While on SES as measured by
total family income there is some variation, the crudeness
of this measure denies a meaningful application to this analysis of commissioner-staff relationships.

Detachable resources include both external bases of
power and acquired knowledge or expertise. The hypothesis
would be that the greater the commission member strength
in detachable resources, vis-à-vis the executive director,
the more likelihood of a Commissioner-Dominant role relationship set. In terms of external bases of power, "detachable resources" are operationalized here as reported
degree of involvement in the women's movement, in community affairs, and in politics. Acquired knowledge or expertise is operationalized by years of formal education and
reputed expertise in an area of commission concern.

Specific contingency situations refer to strategic decision points in a commission's life. The hypothesis here
is that during "the handling of major phase problems, or
strategic decision points ... board power is most likely to
be asserted." "Even if the board is but a rubber stamp,"
Zald notes, "such periods allow some reinforcement of the
image of board power."[15] The strategic decision points
focused on here are, first, an identification crisis occa-
sioned by the elected officials' decision to place a women's
center under a commission staff in one community, and
second, by the event of choosing a chief executive successor
in another community.

Detachable resources lend themselves more readily
to quantitative treatment than do contingency situations.
Here we will analyze this first set of influences on board
power in an effort to illuminate the basis for the types of
board-staff relationships found in four of the five communities studied. [16] Next we turn to contingency situations to
illuminate transitions in the nature of board-staff relationships perceived legitimate over time.

The external power-base indicators of community involvement, political involvement, women's-movement involv-
ment, were ascertained by three questions, each asking commission members and executive officers to locate themselves
on a one-to-ten scale in terms of "degree of involvement,"
with ten reflecting the highest level of involvement. Commissioner responses were then totaled and the mean score
calculated. Since one might reasonably expect the level of
involvement in each of these areas to vary across the communities for staff and commissioners alike, and since the
focus is on the relative advantage of commissioners versus
staff in each of these areas, staff scores on each of the
questions were subtracted from the mean commission score
for that community. The resulting figures shown in the
first three rows of the score column on Table 1 indicate
the degree of advantage or disadvantage of commissioners
versus staff in terms of these resources.

As Table 1 indicates, the Dodge commissioners, with
a .5 difference ratio were the most advantaged vis-à-vis
their staff on the "community involvement" resource. Marysville, with a positive difference ratio of 3.9, appeared the
strongest vis-à-vis staff on the "political involvement" measure. Finally, in terms of women's-movement involvement
all of the commissioner groups appeared somewhat disad-

Table 1

Commissioner Rating on Resources by Community

Commissions

Detachable Resources	Marysville		Dodge		Onega		St. George	
	Score	Rank	Score	Rank	Score	Rank	Score	Rank
Community Involvement	-.5 (n=12)*	2	+.5 (n=19)	1	-1.3 (n=31)	4	-1.2 (n=7)	3
Political Involvement	3.9 (n=12)	1	3.4 (n=19)	2	.3 (n=31)	3	-2.5 (n=7)	4
Women's Movement Involvement	-3.9 (n=12)	4	-1.4 (n=19)	1	-2.2 (n=31)	2	-2.6 (n=7)	3
Education	0 (n=12)	4	53.9 (n=19)	2	64.6 (n=31)	1	28.6 (n=7)	3
Expertise	75 (n=6)	1	11 (n=6)	3	75 (n=7)	1	40 (n=7)	2

*Number of commissioners on which measure is based.

Rank Totals	12	9	11	15
Rank Order Score=	3rd	1st	2nd	4th

vantaged vis-à-vis staff, but Dodge, with its -1.4 difference ratio, appears the least disadvantaged.

The acquired characteristics of knowledge and expertise also serve as a source of board strength. Here again, since the overall resources of both commissioners and staff might be expected to reflect characteristics of the broader community, focus remains on board-staff differences. For education, commissioner scores are ascertained by calculating the percentage of commissioners with years of education at least equivalent to that of the executive director. The higher the percentage score, the stronger the board in terms of education. Here, Onega, where 64.6 percent of the commissioners had attained a level of education equivalent to the chief

staff person, appeared to present the most advantaged commissioner group.   Finally, expertise of commissioners was
gauged by recording the percentage of women among the
commission leadership group (officers of CSW and heads of
major committees) who were designated as experts in some
area of commission concern by the others in the leadership
group and the staff.   As Table 1 shows, Marysville and Onega tied for top place, with 75 percent of the leadership
group judged by their peers as experts.

Having calculated scores on each variable for each
community, we must still ask the question, "Do these differences in detachable resources of members actually correlate with differences in commission-staff role relationships?"   Some summary measure of commissioner strength
is necessary in order to examine this relationship.   Since
there is no a priori justification for any particular weight-
ing scheme among these resources, all five commission
characteristics are weighted equally, and commissions are
ranked from one to five on each variable according to the
degree of commissioner strength signified.   The crudeness
of this calculation is acknowledged.   Simple rankings one
through four disguise the substantial variation in degree of
commissioner-staff difference across commissions.   Still,
it does provide a vehicle for gaining preliminary insight
into the relationship between commissioner-resources and
role-relationship sets.   On community involvement of commissioners, Dodge scored first (.5); Marysville, second
(-.5); St. George, third (-1.2); and Onega, fourth (-1.3).
The ranking for each commission on each of the variables
is indicated in the Rank Column in Table 1.   Adding the
commission ranking on each variable yields a rough summary measure of the commissioners' strength vis-à-vis
the staff across the commissions: the lower the overall
score, the higher the commission on relative commissioner
resources.

The rank-order scores indicate that Dodge represents the commission with the greatest board strength, fol-
lowed by Onega, second, and then Marysville, third.   St.
George represents the case of least board strength.

The hypothesis on the relationship between board
strength in terms of detachable resources and role relationships on the commission gains support with this data.
In Dodge, where the board scored highest on detachable resources, we find a deferring role orientation on the part of

the executive director, and a more controlling role orientation on the part of the commission leadership.   In St. George,
where commission members score lowest on amount of detachable resources, we find an executive officer with a
strong controlling orientation, accompanied by a commission
leadership group more inclined towards sharing control with
staff.

To understand more fully the precise locations of
Marysville and Onega, two commissions falling between the
high and low on commission resources, a second factor,
"strategic contingency situations," becomes useful.   The objective balance of resources between commissioners and
staff can be influenced either by altering the level of resources represented by the commissions or by altering the
resources brought to the commission by the person in the
staff role.   As Zald[17] notes, the occasion of choosing an
executive successor is a time of particular board strength.
Part of that strength resides in the board capacity to alter
what may be perceived as a negative balance of commissioner-staff resources.

Some months before these interviews were conducted,
the commission leadership in Onega exerted its strength at
a time when a new executive director was being selected,
to choose a person who, in terms of the resources brought
to the job, seemed less powerful than her predecessor.
Though complete data were not available on the former executive director, information volunteered during commissioner interviews suggested that on at least two measures
of resource strength, education and apparent women's-movement involvement, the predecessor scored higher than the
commissioner mean.   The commissioners' selection of a
new executive director allowed reassertion of relative board
strength.   This contingency situation illuminates the seeming incongruence between commissioner resources and role
relationships plotted on Figure 1.   The commissioners are
reflecting a view of role relationships that they have had a
hand in creating, a view that generally mirrors a newly
gained relative strength in detachable resources.   The new
executive director, on the other hand, while recognizing
some need to pull back from the reputedly extreme controlling orientation of her predecessor, still bases her notion
of the job on the past executive director's model and, hence,
in her "sharing control" perspective, may be more control
oriented than the objective distribution of resources warrants.

The Marysville commission ranks third on commis-

sioner resources, yet in terms of pure commission activity
fits an almost perfect Commissioner-Dominant ideal. This
seeming anomaly is somewhat clarified by recognition of a
second "contingency situation." Zald has suggested that
"identification" or "character" crises provide an occasion
for a board to assert itself. The inauguration of a women's
center by the county, and the placement of this center under
the staff of the CSW, was the occasion for the Marysville
CSW crisis period. In this case, board reassertion emerged
in the commissioners' call for examination of the "true purpose of the Commission on the Status of Women." Though,
in fact, there had been considerable concern for at least
three years that the staff had grown too powerful, there had
never been a specific issue around which all commissioners
could organize their disgruntlement. The inauguration by
the county of a women's center directed by commission staff
provided the occasion. The upshot of the crisis was that
commissioners seemed to have been granted by the staff
total control over commission policy--a degree of autonomy
that we might not expect to reside in a commission with
such an unfavorable ratio of resources. In exchange, the
existing control of the staff over the budget and the personnel of the women's center was fully acknowledged by the
commissioners. Both commissioners and staff reported
satisfaction with this informal division of control.

Value Congruence Between Commissioners and Staff:
Programmatic and Issue Values

        One of the reasons that the roles played by CSW
staff and commission members assume such central importance is that staff and commission values are not necessarily congruent. Where congruence is not the case, the
nonaccountable staff might be subverting the will of a politically representative womens' commission by following
its own lights. This section considers both the scope of
differences in values between CSW members and staff, and
the implications of those differences for commissioner orientation toward staff role.

        At least two different kinds of values become rele-
vant in this context: programmatic values and issue values.
Programmatic values refer to the general kinds of goal activity in which commissions are engaged. (Goal activity refers here to the means through which organizations attempt
to achieve their "intended state of affairs."[18]) Issue values

refer to the substantive policy issues commissions chose to
stress. Here, commission leadership and staff were asked
to indicate the importance (on a five-point scale) they assigned to commission activity in each of seven goal-activity
areas, and twenty substantive-issue areas. The goal-activity
areas for commissions and the substantive issues with which
they might be concerned are listed in Table 2.

Table 2

Goal Activities and Issue Concerns of Local CSW

Goal Areas

    Public Education/Consciousness Raising
    Needs Assessment
    "Watchdog"/Investigation
    Expansion of Political Participation/Women
    Direct Influence in Local/State/Federal Policy-Making
    Convenor/Catalyst
    Direct Support Services

Substantive-Issue Areas

Education and Training	ERA
Employment	Family Planning
Child Care	Female Offenders
Health Care	Abortion
Political Participation of	Sexual Preference
Women	Battered Women
Credit	Self-Assertiveness/Psychol-
Insurance	ogy of Women
Tax Law	Consciousness Raising on
Housing	Media
Rape	Ethnic Minority Issues
	Legal Rights in Marriage
	and Family

    For each commission, the mean score provided by
the commissioners as a group was calculated for each activity area and issue concern. The commission mean responses and the response of the chief staff officer were then

each ranked by order of importance for both the activity
area and the issue concerns.   In each CSW the relationship
between these two rankings for both activity area and issue
concerns was calculated to provide a summary measure
(Spearman Correlation Coefficient [rho]) of the congruence
between commissioners and staff in each commission on the
relative importance of goal activity areas and substantive
issue concerns.   The higher the correlation between commissioner and staff, the higher the degree of congruence.
Table 3 presents commissions with degree of commissioner-
staff value congruence scores in each of these areas.

    The first point illustrated by Table 3 is that in all
four commissions there was substantially greater commissioner-staff congruence on importance assigned to issues
than on importance assigned to goal activities of commissions.
This may be a result of the fact that staff in general is more

Table 3

Commissioner-Staff Congruence on Value Priorities

Commission	Congruence Scores	
	Goal Activities	Issues
	(n=7)	(n=20)
Marysville	.21	.84
Onega	-.43	.81
Dodge	.57	.81
St. George	.66	.61

willing to take direction from commissioners in setting the
issue agenda, yet more independent when it comes to strategies for acting on issues named on that agenda.   In other
words, staff may want to determine for itself the kinds of
actions that are most fitting to promote shared values in
each of the substantive policy areas.

    Examining the nature of substantive differences in val-
ues about the importance of goal activities is instructive in

this context, for it suggests that, in the main, there is no
standard set of staff priorities.   The only seemingly pat-
terned difference in commissioner-staff priorities across the
four commissions was in the area of needs assessment.
Here the needs-assessment activity area was ranked higher
in importance by staff then by commissioners in three of
the four commissions--a tendency that might be expected,
given the superior capacity of staff to function in this area.

Value Congruence and Role Orientation

        The degree of value congruence between commissioners
and staff is important to analyze in its own right.   Additionally, this analysis is important for the light it sheds on the
role orientation of commissioners.   One recent study of California coastal commissions tested a thesis derived from
Gamson's[19] assertion that "value congruence produces trust."
This study concluded that "by far the best predictor of commissioner views concerning the extent to which staff should
take an active role in policy-making is the degree to which
they agree with staff on basic policy issues."[20]

        To test this hypothesis in the CSW context, we must
distinguish between congruence on goal-activity areas and
substantive policy issues, since, as noted above, there is
no one-to-one relationship between staff-commissioner congruence in each of these value areas.   Still, consistent with
the value-congruence thesis, we would expect that the greater the value congruence in each area, the greater commission leadership's willingness to defer to staff; the lower the
value congruence, the greater commission leadership desire
to control, exclusive of staff.[21]

        Table 4 presents the four commissions ranked by com-
missioner deference to staff, staff-commissioner congruence
on goal-activity areas, and staff-commissioner congruence
on issues.

        The hypothesis of a relationship between commissioner
orientation toward staff role and congruence on policy issues
is not supported by these data.   The commission with the
lowest score on policy-issue congruence, St. George, rated
highest on commissioner deference to staff.   The other commissions grouped together closely in terms of value congruence in a pattern seemingly unrelated to role orientation.
The value-congruence hypothesis gains support,   however,

Table 4

A Comparison of Commission Rankings by Commissioner
Deference, Goal Activities, and Issues

Rank	Commissioner Deference	Goal Activities	Issues
(1)	St. George	St. George (.66)*	Marysville (.84)
(2)	Dodge	Dodge (.57)	Onega (.81)
(3)	Marysville a**	Marysville (.21)	Dodge (.81)
(4)	Onega	Onega (-.43)	St. George (.66)

*Spearman's rho.
**Marysville a is selected to represent the Marysville CSW here
due to its more general CSW charge.

when one focuses on goal-activity-area values.   In St. George
the commissioners expressed the least controlling orientation
toward staff and show the highest congruence on functions.
Dodge and Marysville a ranked second and third on commissioner deference and fit, as well, second and third in congruence on functional-activity areas.   Onega, where commissioners and staff expressed the lowest congruence on
functions, exhibited the most controlling-oriented commissioners.   Of course, it is important to stress that in all
commissions, with the exception of women's-center component of Marysville, commissioners believed that their roles
should range from sharing with staff to controlling.   No
commissioners advocated entirely deferring to staff across
the board.   Still, differences in controlling orientations are
evident and do seem clearly associated with the presence
and absence of value congruence on functional goal-activity
areas.

Conclusion

This paper has examined a type of citizen's commission that has come to play a central role in the community-
level women's movement in many jurisdictions across the
country--the Commission on the Status of Women.   Five
commissions, perceived as particularly successful, serve
as the basis of this study.

First, a typology based on the role orientations of commissioners and staff was posited. The five commissions were described against the background of this typology. Interview material fleshed out the meaning assigned by commissioners and staff to each of the three role-relationship types appearing in this group of commissions. Next, the association between board characteristics and role relationships was discussed. Analyzing four of the five commissions, we found support for Zald's hypothesis that both commissioners' "detachable resources" and "strategic contingency situations" in the life of a commission have positive impact on board power over staff. Finally, actual value congruence of commissioners and executive directors was explored in four CSW. Substantial congruence was found between commissioners and staff on the importance of substantive issues across commissions. However, commissions varied greatly on the congruence between commissioners and staff on importance assigned to goal-activity areas. Support emerged as well for the hypothesis that commissioner willingness to share control over decision making with staff is positively related to staff-commissioner congruence on importance assigned to goal activities of the commission.

On a practical level, what do these findings suggest about the significance of staff growth for local Commissions on the Status of Women? At this point at least a few guidelines, offered from the commissioner's perspective, merit emphasis. First, commissioners should not expect their role perceptions to be shared automatically by staff. An executive director's perspectives are shaped by a variety of influences, including the experiences she brings to the job as well as her understanding of her predecessor's role. Second, commissioners may need to plan more deliberately for the kind of CSW they would like to see in their community. If founders believe that a CSW should be citizen dominant, they should not select an executive director with substantial "detachable resources" and must be willing to adjust their expectation of her accordingly. Third, commissioners might reflect on the finding that agreement between commissioners and staff on a substantive-issue agenda does not imply agreement on the goal activities or the intended results of commission action. Compatible sets of role expectations might flow from agreement on what the Commission on the Status of Women should be doing but may be unrelated to issue agenda. Accordingly, a firmer hand by commission leadership in shaping the initial goal-activity plan might reduce dysfunctional conflict.

Finally in a more speculative vein, one might conclude that since perfect compatibility between commissioner
and staff role definitions occurred in only one of the reputedly effective commissions, it simply may not be an essential
ingredient of success.   This interpretation is buttressed by
the fact that the sole case of perfect compatibility was Altona, where staff support was minimal.   If one views Commissions on the Status of Women as essentially process institutions, whose criterion of success is the extent to which
they maintain opportunity for open expression of a wide range
of women's preferences, the centrality of staff-commissioner
role compatibility becomes suspect.   In other words, one
might conclude that, to the extent "controlling activity" is
associated with intense interest and concern on the part of
the participants, "the more the better" inclusive of commissioners and staff might be the best rule to follow.   A
second-level staff person in one commission suggested that
for a commission to be effective there may have to be
strength in both staff and commission:

> Then you have strong personalities and you have
> people vying for power and leadership, so there's
> inevitably going to be tension.   So I'd say ... it's
> probably endemic--you can't have an effective com-
> mission without having this kind of power struggle
> going on.

Notes

[1]Norman Kerr, "The School Board as an Agency of
Legitimation," Sociology of Education 38 (Fall 1964):   39-
59; L. Harmon Zeigler and M. Kent Jennings, Governing
American Schools (North Scituate, Mass.:   Duxbury, 1974);
Alan Altshuler, A Land Use Plan for St. Paul, ICP #90
(Indianapolis: Bobbs-Merrill, 1965); Irving Schiffman, The
Limits of the Local Planning Commission (Davis, Calif.:
Institute of Governmental Affairs, 1975); Oliver Williams
and Charles Adrian, Four Cities (Philadelphia: University
of Pennsylvania Press, 1963); John DeGrove, The Florida
Flood Control District, ICP #58 (Indianapolis: Bobbs-Mer-
rill, 1960); and Dale Rogers Marshall, The Politics of Par-
ticipation in Poverty (Berkeley: University of California
Press, 1971).
[2]James Q. Wilson, Political Organizations (New York:
Basic Books, 1973).
[3]Paul Sabatier and Daniel Mazmanian, "Relationships

Between Part-Time Policy-Makers and Full-Time Staffs:
The California Coastal Commissions." Paper presented at
the Annual Meeting of the Midwest Political Science Association, Chicago, April 20-22, 1978.

4Organizational data presented here on the population
of local CSW were coded directly from questionnaires returned in response to a Women's Bureau survey (U.S. Department of Labor) in the summer of 1975. Officially, there
were seventy-five local commissions at that time. About
sixty of these maintained some level of activity; forty-eight
of these functioning commissions responded to the Women's
Bureau survey.

5The District of Columbia Commission was not included in this study because it was viewed by some of the panel
members as closer to a state commission than a local commission in its operation and self-conception.

6"U.S. National Women's Agenda," Social Policy, VI
(March/April, 1976): 24-25.

7John C. Wahlke et al., The Legislative System (New
York: John Wiley, 1962).

8Ibid.

9A. Paul Hare, Handbook of Small Group Research,
2nd ed. (New York: Free Press, 1976).

10Herbert Kaufman, "Emerging Conflicts in the Doc-
trines of Public Administration," American Political Science
Review 50 (1956): 1057-1073.

11Zeigler and Jennings, Governing American Schools.

12The literature focusing on organizational styles would
characterize this as the "retired-on-the-job" style (Lau,
1975: 38). The consequence of this style if adopted by
organizational leaders is that the organization will be unable
to cope with changes in the environment and will be heavily
committed to the status quo.

13Mayer Zald, "The Power and Functions of Boards of
Directors: A Theoretical Synthesis," American Journal of
Sociology 75 (July 1969): 97-111.

14Ibid.

15Ibid., p. 107.

16Due to the difficulty of interpreting the resource balance given the very limited commitment of the Altona staff,
this case is excluded from analysis.

17Zald, "The Power and Functions of Boards of Directors."

18Lawrence B. Mohr, "The Concept of Organizational
Goal," American Political Science Review 63 (June 1973): 470-
481.

19William Gamson, Power and Discontent (Homewood,
Ill.: Dorsey, 1968).

[20]Sabatier and Mazmanian, "Relationships."

[21]The hypothesis is premised on the assumption that commissioners correctly perceive staff value orientations and respond to those in formulating their orientations toward their respective roles.   The data, however, are on staff and commissioner attitudes, not perceptions of each others' attitudes.   Since there is a substantial amount of interaction between commission leadership and the executive director, there is strong reason to believe that commissioners can perceive actual attitudes of staff.   Sabatier and Mazmanian (1978) make a similar assumption.

PERCEPTIONS OF WOMEN'S ROLES ON LOCAL COUNCILS IN CONNECTICUT

Susan Gluck Mezey

Studies of the psychology of group behavior show that different relationships between the sexes emerge when there are different proportions of men and women in the groups.[1] One study of women in a corporate setting indicates that interaction among the members of the groups is affected by the relative number of women in a particular setting. The observation of women in a nondomestic setting often evokes discussion of the marginality of the female actors in the male-dominated environment.[2] Marginal people are those caught between two roles and wanting to belong to both, yet not fully belonging to either. Marginal members of a group are subject to role strain and conflicting role identities. Typically there is a power struggle involved, since marginality "implies superior status of one group and the minority status of another [and] the marginal one is stigmatized and excluded from positions of power by the dominant one."[3]

Tokenism often results from the pressure of the marginal group attempting to break into the world dominated by the majority group. Although Kanter refers to tok-

ens as merely the members of the outgroup, the term takes
on a symbolic meaning as well.

> Tokenism is the means by which the dominant
> group advertises a promise of mobility between
> the dominant and excluded classes. By definition,
> however, tokenism involves mobility which is
> severely restricted in quantity and the quality
> of mobility is severely restricted as well. The
> Token does not become assimilated into the dom-
> inant group but is destined for permanent mar-
> ginality. The Token is a member of an under-
> represented group who is operating on the turf
> of the dominant group, under license from it. [4]

When women, or any outgroup, exists as a minority
of the dominant group, they may develop reactive responses,
such as increased awareness of the differences between the
two groups, or they may identify with the dominant group
and attempt to remove themselves from identification with
the subordinate group. [5] Perceptions of their acceptance
may be at variance, and dominants tend to ignore or dis-
count the hardships suffered by the tokens as a result of
their marginal status.

Public office is one area where women operate in
a minority setting and are potentially subject to problems
arising from marginality and tokenism. While women are
becoming increasingly more evident in political office at
all levels, little is known about their ability to function as
members of their political organizations. There is a great
deal written of the recruitment experiences of female politicians, and some attention has been paid to issue preferences and policy orientations; however, the role of women
in public office, particularly the special problems and difficulties peculiar to political women, has not been systematically analyzed. Little attention has been paid to personality factors that hinder or help women cope with the role
strain resulting from their marginal positions, nor to the
interaction between men and women in public office and
their differing perceptions of the way women play the political game.

Most studies of the attitudes and behavior of political
women are interesting and informative about individual feel-
ings involved and tell how women reacted to certain problems arising from role strain and marginality; however,

since they are limited to samples of women only, no comparative male-female perspective is possible, and because they are largely biographical and anecdotal, it is difficult to generalize from them.[6] In these analyses there is little attempt to explore whether perceptions of female political actors held by females are different from those held by male political actors and whether there are sex differences in norms of female political behavior.

This study addresses itself to these questions by examining the role of women in public office in the state of Connecticut and determining whether perceptions of these roles differ according to sex. Since the literature on marginality stresses the importance of the relative number of marginal actors in a group dominated by the majority, this analysis will also determine whether perceptions of females in public office are affected by the number of women holding office together in a particular setting. The literature on marginality and tokenism and groups with memberships of sex-skewed ratios leads to the expectation that both questions will be answered affirmatively.

Connecticut Local Office*

Because women constitute a much smaller proportion of political-office holders than men, they typically serve as minorities or sole members of legislative bodies. Although local governments have always offered women the greatest opportunity to serve as public officials, women still remain underrepresented in this area as well. It is often argued that women seek local political office because they are more easily accepted at this level by voters who assume women are closer to traditional local concerns.[7] Evidence exists that people are more likely to support female candidates for positions that conform to the female stereotype, such as school-board membership.[8] Local office is more congenial to women also, since many of the problems inherent in holding public office at the state and national level do not pertain at this level.[9] Whatever the reason, statistically the percentage of women officeholders is higher at the municipal level than at the state or federal

*The discussion of the context and data base for this research was presented in the Mezey article in Part I of this volume. It is reintroduced here for reader convenience.

level. Local public office therefore offers an attractive position to examine perceptions of women holding office and
to discover whether these perceptions vary with the number
of women holding office together on a particular council.

Connecticut is a good site for the study of local wom-
en because it has proven to be somewhat more congenial
than other states to the elected woman public official. Connecticut women constitute roughly 13 percent of local legis-
lators--slightly higher than the national average of about
10 percent. Possibly the state's greater acceptance of wom-
en officeholders, also seen in the relatively high percentage
of women state legislators (20.3 percent in 1977), encourages
more women to run for office. Connecticut's particular form
of local government or party organization (nominees to local
office are selected by the town committee in each town) may
also be responsible for the greater participation of women
in local government.

Connecticut is also particularly well suited for a
study of local government since political participation among
its citizens is closely tied to town meetings and local legislative governing bodies in the 169 towns within the state.
Town governments represent an important part of community
life; recently the state has even increased its efforts to "encourage effective local services and to strengthen the financial ability of towns to provide these services."[10] Eight
towns still conform to the original New England town-meeting model, while the remainder have adapted the model to
suit their particular needs. All municipalities are governed
today by legislative bodies; these range from a three-member Board of Selectman to a forty-seat Town Council.

Women in Local Office: The Sample

Fifty female politicians were randomly selected to
be interviewed from towns and cities in Connecticut that
had women representatives on the local legislative bodies;
the selection was based upon a stratified random sample
according to the size of the municipality. Personal interviews lasting from one-half hour to two hours were conducted with each respondent. A corresponding sample of fifty
male officeholders was also interviewed. To focus on sex
differences, we matched the males to the women by town,
age, and party affiliation; when possible, respondents were
also matched by length of time in office. The matching

procedure was relaxed when circumstances required as in
small towns with a three-member Board of Selectmen; in
every case, however, females and their matched male respondents were members of the same board or council.   As
illustrated in Table 1, representatives from forty-one Town
Councils were included in the survey.

Table 1

Selection of the Sample

Population of Municipality	Number of Women Sampled[a]	Number of Municipalities Sampled[b]
Under 5,000	5	5
5,001 to 15,000	11	10
15,001 to 25,000	12	12
25,001 to 50,000	6	5
Over 50,000	16	9

[a]Men were selected from the same towns as the women.

[b]More than one woman representative was selected in the following
municipalities: Monroe (2); Manchester (2); Danbury (2); New Haven
(3); Waterbury (2); and Stamford (4).   The municipalities were divided into five size categories according to their populations and
the number of women from each of the five groups was calculated
as a percentage of the total number of women in office; this percentage was then computed as a percentage of the total sample
size.   The female officeholders were numbered and randomly chos-
en from a table of random numbers until the five groups were each
filled.   Women who declined to be interviewed were replaced by
the next random number in their group.

A comparison of the ages and number of years in
office as well as the party affiliations shows that the matching attempts were successful.   The average age of women
respondents was 47.3; for men, 45.4; the average number
of years in office was three for the women and 3.5 years
for the men.   Thirty-one women and thirty-four men were
Democrats, eighteen women and fifteen men were Republicans; one woman and one man were each members of a locally based conservative party.

Although there was one larger city council where as

many as ten women served together, about half the councils in
the survey (twenty) had only one woman on them. The rest
ranged from two women together to five sitting in one council
chamber. The mean percentage of women in the forty-one
councils included in the survey was 24 percent; there were
roughly four to five men to every woman on a council (the
mean ratio was 4.6 to 1). The average number of women
on each council was 2.8.

Perceptions of Equal Opportunity on Town Councils

Perceptions of the role of marginals or tokens in
office often revolve around questions of acceptance of the
minority members by the dominants in a social and professional setting as well as the ability of the minority to function effectively in their surroundings. Although some women
politicians perceive advantages because of their unique position within politics, most observers of the political opportunity structure note a bias within political institutions that
denies women the same opportunities as men to assume positions of political influence.[11] Furthermore, while sex is
not generally related to policy preference, it is related to
attitudes about women in office and concern for equal opportunity for women in elite roles.[12]

At least one study of perceptions of women officeholders found sex differences in attitudes toward women
politicians: men were more inclined to underestimate problems that women encountered and more inclined to believe
the problems stemmed from personal inadequacies rather
than systemic bias. Women were more apt to point out
obstacles placed in their paths and blame these obstacles
on their environment and their male colleagues.[13] In sum,
although political women express confidence in themselves
and their ability to succeed in their political roles, they
are cognizant of burdens imposed upon them because of
their sex.

When questioned about equal opportunity in Connecticut local offices, the majority of female and male respondents agreed women have to work extra hard to prove their
capabilities but felt that sex was not an important and certainly not insurmountable hindrance to the effectiveness of
women as political actors. Most believed women were not
unduly burdened by special problems. Disagreement arose
over the degree of difficulty that sex imposes on female
politicos. Table 2 compares male and female attitudes

toward the effectiveness of women officeholders and their
opportunities for political power.

Table 2

Perceptions of Equal Opportunity for
Women in Local Office By Sex[a]

Measures of Equal Opportunity	% Women Agree (n = 50)	% Men Agree (n = 50)
Sex hinders the effectiveness of women on local councils.	20	12
Women are as likely as men to accumulate power on local councils.	62	62
Women on local councils have to work extra hard to prove them- selves to their male colleagues.*	82	42
Women have a great deal of dif- ficulty moving up into the hierarchy of leadership in state politics.**	56	24
Women in local government have special problems which diminish their effectiveness.	32	20
Women have same opportunities as men to get elected to local public office.	66	80

[a]Unless noted, relationships are not significant at the .05 level.

*Phi=.41 ($p < .001$).

**Phi=.32 ($p < .01$).

As the table indicates, women are less sanguine about
the opportunities available to them; women were less op-
timistic about their potential influence and more willing to
believe greater liabilities existed for them than for men.
While these questions focused on women in local office, sex
differences also appeared in their attitudes about women in
politics in the abstract without mention of a particular level
or kind of office. Men were far less likely to believe women
were subjected to discriminatory treatment on the basis of
sex. Table 3 illustrates these attitudes and shows that perceptions of women in local office are consistent with those

of women at other levels of office. The Connecticut politicians
are similar to those discussed in other studies in terms of
recognition of a bias against women and sex differences in
perceptions of that bias.

Table 3

Perceptions of Liabilities
of Women Politicians by Sex[a]

Perception of Liability	% Women Agree (n = 50)	% Men Agree (n = 50)
Women have special liabilities in campaigns.	52	58
Women in office have special liabilities.	34	36
Women are not inside the smoke-filled rooms with men.	24	18
Party hierarchy is last to see woman's potential even when she has strong base of support.*	46	22*
Women can never get to inner circles of power.**	40	12
A woman has to be twice as good as a man to succeed in politics.***	60	30
Women get most of the dirty-work chores in politics while men hold the real power.****	54	32

[a]Unless noted, relationships are not significant at the .05 level.

* Phi=.25 (p < .05).   ***Phi=.30 (p < .01).
**Phi=.31 (p < .01).   ****Phi. =.22 (p < .05).

Social Integration of Political Women

Social interaction is often considered an important part
of a politician's behavior in office. Since many decisions are
made outside the formal meetings and conferences, it is necessary to learn whether women attend the informal gatherings
as well as the prescribed meetings. Other studies of fe-

male politicians report that women tend to feel isolated from
men in extracurricular activities and do not participate as fully
as men in nonofficial events. [14]

These local politicians appear generally convinced of
the importance of social relationships as a part of their official
responsibilities; the women are even more committed than the
men and the majority of both sexes report engaging in informal
activities with their political colleagues. However, as Table
4 shows, there was a difference of opinion about whether wom-
en suffer from sexual segregation in political life.

Table 4

Views on Social Integration
of Local Women Politicians by Sex[a]

Perception of Social Interaction	% Women Agree (n = 50)	% Men Agree (n = 50)
Informal activities are im-portant to politicians' work.	92	84
Discusses political business at informal gatherings.	88	90
Women are likely to be frozen out of informal political contacts.	28	12
Women are fully included in in-formal political contacts.*	48	80

[a]Unless noted, relationships are not significant at the .05 level.

*Phi=.33 (p < .01).

Although the majority of women and men report that wom-
en are not frozen out of the informal interaction among councilmembers, the women seemed somewhat less sure. When asked
whether women were "fully included," the female politicians
were much less convinced of their equal social status.

Personality Traits Among Women in Politics

The explanation for the scarcity of women in politics is
that they lack necessary personality traits that are commonly
found in male politicians. Although women politicians do not

draw these conclusions, they also report a belief in personality
differences and behavior patterns between themselves and their
male colleagues. [15] The theory of personality differences between the sexes is reported in other studies: female political elites are reputed to have different concerns from
men, which stem from personality differences. [16] In a
study of personality traits among elected politicians, males
were described as more "self-assured" and "self-controlled,"
while women were reputed to be more "assertive" and "im-
aginative." [17] The authors concluded these were qualities
that "appeared to be major assets in their success in a
political role that is powerful, but also contradictory to
sex-role expectations." [18]

     Political women are often placed in the difficult po-
sition of being forced to assume "masculine," i.e., successful, personality traits while retaining the image of a typical
"feminine" personality.   Their marginal status as women
politicians imposes these contradictory sex-role norms.
This problem is exemplified in a study of the 1963-1964
Connecticut State Legislature that placed most female legislators in the "spectator" group.   The group consisted of
those with little ambition or sense of individuality and highly sensitive to approval or disapproval from others. [19]

     In the more than ten years since the state legislator
study it is likely that sex differences in personality traits
would be somewhat less pronounced and attitudes towards
women politicians would be somewhat less negative.   When
asked about personality traits among women politicians, the
local politicians in the sample did not subscribe to the view
that women were inferior per se or unable to handle their
political responsibilities.   As Table 5 illustrates there was
a good deal of agreement about personality differences between the sexes.   Although a large majority agreed that
women in public office are as "logical and rational" as men,
more than half the women and the men felt that political
women are "usually more idealistic" than men; almost half
the men and one-quarter of the women believed most men
are "better suited emotionally" for political activities.   Similarly, almost half believed that women are more "sensitive," "attach greater value to human life," and have more
"artistic ability" than men, while more than half thought
"feminine charm and diplomacy" can be a woman politician's
greatest assets.   As might be expected, women were less
likely to adopt the position that women were less able to
succeed in public life because of sex differences in personality traits.

Table 5

Perceptions of Sex Differences
in Personality Traits by Sex[a]

Personality Traits	% Women Agree (n = 50)	% Men Agree (n = 50)
Women are more sensitive to problems of poor and under-privileged than men are.	56	40
Women have more artistic ability than men do.	26	40
Men are better at economics and business than women.	22	38
Women attach greater value to human life than men do.	44	40
Feminine charm and diplomacy can be a woman politician's greatest assets.	60	56
Most men are better suited emotionally for politics than most women.	24	42
Women in public office can be just as logical and rational as men.	98	90
Women in politics are usually more idealistic than men.	64	54

[a]Unless noted, relationships are not significant at the .05 level.

Representation

Representation is a recurring theme in the discussion of the roles that women politicians play in public life. The relationship between women politicians and women in society is an integral part of this theme; the question if often asked whether women are elected to office with a special mandate to represent women's interests, however those interests might be defined in a particular community.

This concept of representation, defined by Hannah Pitkin as "descriptive representation" assumes that women in public

office are consciously motivated to speak for women's issues. [20]
An elected official who is "like" the people she or he represents is said to "stand for" that group; the likeness is usually defined by race, color, ethnic origin, or sex.   Pitkin
also introduces the concept of "acting for" to expand upon
descriptive representation.   When a representative acts for
a group in society, she or he is working for the benefit of
the group, responding to pressure from it, and pursuing its
welfare.   Although the two notions of descriptive representation do not have to coalesce in one elected official, there
is usually an expectation that this will occur.   The efforts
of various minority-group members to increase the number
of "like" politicians attests to the universality of this belief.

     Women also cling to this tenet, and one of the cor-
nerstones of feminist policy is the election of more women
to public office as symbolic of power and influence within
the system and as an asset in implementing women's political interests.   The policy is predicated upon the conviction,
or at least hope, that women politicians will assume special
responsibility for the passage of legislation to further the
interests of women in society.   Furthermore, feminists
argue that women constituents expect female politicians to
fulfill these obligations.   Table 6 shows that women politicians in Connecticut local offices are in accord with this
position, much more so than the men.   All but one feel
that women in politics set an example to women in society,
and a large majority believe that political women should take
leading positions on women's issues.   These women politicians are generally convinced that women "out there" expect them to do so and that they have a special responsibility to their female constituents.   The men in the sample
were far less convinced of these matters.   Not surprisingly,
men were also much less disturbed about the number of
women politicians.

     It might be supposed that feminism and sympathy for
the women's movement are responsible for positive attitudes
toward representation of women's issues and commitment
to more women in politics; Table 7 shows that such is not
the case.   The correlations of these views with feminist
leanings are uniformly weak and insignificant.   While many
of these Connecticut public officials sanction a strong representative role for women in office and acknowledge a
special link between women in the mass public and women
in office, these views do not stem from a feminist philosophy.   Among these politicians, the notion of representation

Table 6

Attitudes Toward Representation
by Women Politicians by Sex[a]

Views on Women Politicians	% Women Agree (n = 50)	% Men Agree (n = 50)
Women in politics serve as examples to women in society.*	98	84
Women politicians have special responsibility to represent the interests of women in society.**	56	12
Women members of local councils should take leading positions on women's issues.	68	48
Women in society look to women in office to take such positions.***	82	62
There are too few women in political office.****	96	62

[a]Unless noted, relationships are not significant at the .05 level

*Phi=.24 (p < .05).

**Phi=.46 (p < .001).

***Phi=.22 (p < .05).

****Phi=.41 (p < .001).

appears nonideological; it probably arises from a vague concern for women's "interests," which are not necessarily political in content.

The Effects of a Sex-Skewed Ratio

Sex plays an important part in determining attitudes toward the role of women in politics; perceptions and norms of women politicians' behavior are greatly influenced by one's sex. The second question raised at the beginning of this study related to numbers of women sitting together; it was expected that perceptions of women's roles in office would be affected by the number of wom-

Table 7

Correlations of Profeminist Attitudes and Views
on Descriptive Representation: Pearson's r

Attitudes toward
Descriptive Representation[a]   Profeminist Attitudes[b]

	Sympathy for WMC[c]	Self-image as feminist[d]
Women as examples	-.07(ns)	-.14(ns)
Special responsibility	.10(ns)	.20(.02)
Leading positions	.12(ns)	-.03(ns)
Expectations of such positions	.02(ns)	-.18(.04)
Number of women in office	-.12(ns)	-.06(ns)

[a] For wording of statement see Table 6; agreement with feminist position coded 1, disagreement coded 2.

[b] Support for feminism coded 1, nonsupport coded 2.

[c] n = 98.

[d] n = 99.

en on a council.   To test this proposition a factor analysis was performed and four factors were extracted.   The factors are comprised of items relating to perceptions of the liabilities, the representation role, social integration, and personality traits of women politicians.   Table 8 shows the items and factor loadings in each factor.   The factor analysis is used as a data reduction device to facilitate further analysis.

Since many variables in each factor were significantly related to sex, it is not surprising that there were significant sex differences in each factor.   Attitudinal variables, such as political-party affiliation or political philosophy, were almost entirely unrelated to the four factors, as were age, education, and income.   Similarly, these perceptions were not associated with size of the municipality nor size of the council.   Political characteristics, such as executive position on the council, number of years in office, and ambition for higher office, were also unrelated to the factors.

These perceptions, typified by each of the four factors, relate to women's roles as minority actors in an environment traditionally male-dominated and usually even defined in male terms, i.e., alderman, councilman, selectman. It is probable that these perceptions vary according to the number of women present on a council; however, there are different ways of obtaining this indicator. In some cases the presence of a woman alone may be more important than the absolute number of women sitting together; in other cases the ratio of men to women or percentage of women of the total council may have a more significant effect on perceptions of women officeholders. Attitudes toward the social integration of women politicians may change as the number of women on a council increases from one to two and bear little relationship to how many women there are altogether; alternatively, attitudes toward the representative role of women in public office may only be influenced by the absolute number of women sitting together. The ratio of men to women and the percentage of women on the council were two other indicators used in the analysis; each tells something different about the relationship between the sexes on a council. A woman alone on a three member board results in a high percentage of women officeholders but subjects her to all potential disadvantages of a sex-skewed ratio. Similarly, a ratio figure alone is insufficient on a large council of twenty or more where there are four or five men to every women but a large number of women sitting together and less vulnerable to isolation or exclusion.

Contrary to expectations, there were no relationships between perceptions of women's roles in office as expressed in the four factors and the number of women sitting together on the council. The hypothesized relationship does not exist among these councilmembers: none of the measures of tokenism or marginality in a sex-skewed ratio affected their perceptions of women's roles. Since it might be expected that men and women are affected differently by the number of women on a council, individual correlations within each sex were performed on the relationships between the four factors and two measures of women on councils: the absolute number of women together and the presence of a woman sitting alone. None of these relationships was significant. Table 9 illustrates these results.

Discussion

The first hypothesis was confirmed, the second was

Table 8

Factors Analysis of Items Relating to Perceptions
of Women Politicians' Roles

Item	Factor I[a]	Factor II	Factor III	Factor IV
Women have same opportunities as men to get elected.	-.75301	.13622	-.08787	-.02691
Women get more of the dirty-work chores.	.58712	-.13478	.41380	.14376
Party does not see women's potential.	.64066	.03688	.28458	-.01474
Sex hinders the effectiveness of women.	.67155	.01523	-.10357	-.20030
Women have special problems.	.58908	.30713	-.11320	.21549
Women politicians should lead on women's interests.	.03561	.80390	.05227	.08619
Women in society expect them to take lead.	-.07343	.69162	.03151	.13408
Women politicians have special responsibility to women in state.	.12940	.50248	.44926	-.33379

Item	Factor I[a]	Factor II	Factor III	Factor IV
Women politicians are frozen out of social interaction.	.04775	.02065	.81665	.02936
Women politicians are fully included.	-.13192	-.16665	-.83123	-.12849
Men are better at economics than women.	.01250	.18571	-.09506	.71879
Political women are more idealistic than men.	.12795	.08858	.29668	.55939
Men are better suited emotionally for politics.	-.09518	-.07148	.04271	.74719
Eigenvalue	3.16390	1.80302	1.50607	1.36721
% of Variance	22.6%	12.9%	10.8%	9.8%
Cumulative%	22.6%	35.5%	46.2%	56.0%

[a]Factor I, Equal Opportunity; Factor II, Representation; Factor III, Social Integration; Factor IV, Personality Traits. Varimax rotated factor matrix.

Table 9

Correlations of Factors and Number of Women
on Local Councils: Pearson's r[a]

Factors	Absolute # of Women	Ratio of Men[b] to Women	% of Women[c]	Presence of[d] Sole Woman
I	-.04(ns)	.03(ns)	.01(ns)	-.09(ns)
II	-.04(ns)	.02(ns)	-.01(ns)	-.07(ns)
III	.06(ns)	-.06(ns)	.04(ns)	.06(ns)
IV	.08(ns)	.04(ns)	-.00(ns)	.04(ns)

	Women Only[e]		Men Only[f]	
Factors	Absolute #	Sole Woman	Absolute #	Sole Woman
I	.01(ns)	-.10(ns)	-.11(ns)	-.09(ns)
II	-.05(ns)	.04(ns)	-.05(ns)	-.19(ns)
III	.12(ns)	.15(ns)	-.01(ns)	.03(ns)
IV	.07(ns)	.03(ns)	.10(ns)	.05(ns)

[a]n = 100.

[b]Ratio = Total number on council divided by number of women together.

[c]Percent = Number of women on council divided by total number on council.

[d]Recoded: Woman alone = 0; 2 women or more = 1.

[e]n = 50.

[f]n = 50.

not. Sex differences in perceptions of women's roles were
apparent in the several dimensions tested: social integration, representation of a female constituency, equal opportunity for women in public office, and personality differences
between the sexes. The women were more cognizant of
their marginal status than the men were; however, neither
felt women could not play the political game successfully.

Even though other studies have suggested that the
number of women in a position affects attitudes toward wom-
en, perceptions of the role of women in public office were
not at all affected by the number of women in that role;
these politicians did not react to a sex-skewed ratio in the
same manner that people in other roles did.

It is difficult to do more than speculate on the reasons for this indifference to the number of women on the
council. Perhaps it doesn't matter how many women serve
on the council, because the women are always in the minority; one could argue that there are simply not enough women
in politics to affect perceptions of their role. It is also
possible that the perceptions are convictions that are not re-
flective of the respondents' experiences on the councils and
would not be affected by observed behavior on the councils. If
the perceptions are not accurate measures of behavior on the
council, they would not necessarily be altered by changes of
council personnel, i.e., more women on it.

To test whether the perceptions of both women and
men change as more women begin to serve as councilmembers and to determine whether these perceptions are actually related to behavior on the councils, time and direct observation are required. Furthermore, additional research
in another locale is necessary to ascertain whether the opinions expressed by these politicians would conform with the
opinions of other politicians--at other levels of office in a
different geographic area.

Notes

[1]Rosabeth Moss Kanter, "Some Effects of Proportions on Group Life: Skewed Sex Ratios and Responses to
Token Women," American Journal of Sociology 28 (March
1977): 965-990; Rosabeth Moss Kanter, "Women and the
Structures of Organizations: Explorations in Theory and
Behavior," in Marcia Millman and Rosabeth Moss Kanter,
eds., Another Voice (Garden City, N.Y.: Anchor Press, 1975).

[2]Judith Lorber, "Women and Medical Sociology: Invisible Professionals and Ubiquitous Patients," in Another Voice; A.K. Daniels, "Feminist Perspectives in Sociological Research," in Another Voice; J. Prather, "Why Can't Women Be More Like Men: A Summary of the Sociopsychological Factors Hindering Women's Advancement in the Professions," in L. Fidell and J. Delameter, eds., Women in the Professions: What's All the Fuss About? (Beverly Hills: Sage, 1971); B. Bass, J. Krusell, and R. Alexander, "Male Managers' Attitudes Toward Working Women," in Women in the Professions; and M. Groszko and R. Morgenstern, "Institutional Discrimination: The Case of Achievement-Oriented Women in Higher Education," in F. Denmark, ed., Who Discriminates Against Women? (Beverly Hills: Sage, 1974).

[3]Joyce J. Walstedt, "Women as Marginals," Psychological Reports 34 (1974): 639-646.

[4]Judith L. Laws, "The Psychology of Tokenism: An Analysis," Sex Roles 1, 1 (1975): 51-67.

[5]Kanter, "Some Effects of Proportions."; Graham Stains, Toby E. Jayaratne, and Carol Tavris, "The Queen Bee Syndrome," Psychology Today 7 (January 1974): 55-60.

[6]Peggy Lamson, Few Are Chosen: American Women in Political Life Today (Boston: Houghton Mifflin, 1968); Hope Chamberlin, A Minority of Members: Women in the U.S. Congress (New York: Praeger, 1973); Susan Tolchin and Martin Tolchin, Clout: Womanpower and Politics (New York: Putnam's, 1973); Irene Diamond, Sex Roles in the State House (New Haven: Yale University Press, 1977); and Jeane Kirkpatrick, Political Woman (New York: Basic Books, 1974).

[7]Edmond Costantini and Kenneth Craik, "Women as Politicians: The Social Background, Personality, and Political Careers of Female Party Leaders," Journal of Social Issues 28, (1972): 217-236.

[8]R. Hedlund, P. Freeman, K. Hamm, and R. Stein, "The Electability of Women Candidates: The Effects of Sex Role Stereotypes." Prepared for the Annual Meeting of the Midwest Political Science Association, Chicago, Illinois, 1978.

[9]S. G. Mezey, "The Effects of Sex on Recruitment: Connecticut Local Offices." Prepared for delivery at the Annual Convention of the Midwest Political Science Association, Chicago, Illinois, 1978.

[10]League of Women Voters, Connecticut in Focus (Connecticut: League of Women Voters of Connecticut Education Fund, 1974).

[11]Diamond, Sex Roles in the State House; Kirkpatrick, Political Woman; Jeane Kirkpatrick, The New Presidential

Elite (New York: Sage, 1977); Tolchin and Tolchin, Clout: Womanpower and Politics; and S. G. Mezey, "Does Sex Make a Difference? A Case Study of Women in Politics," Western Political Quarterly, forthcoming, 1979.
    12B. Cook, "Women's Issues Before Women Judges in the State Trial Courts." Prepared for the Annual Meeting of the Law and Society Association, Minneapolis, Minnesota, 1978; K. Jennings and B. Farah, "Social Roles and Political Resources: An Over-Time Study of Men and Women in Party Elites." Prepared for the Annual Meeting of the Midwest Political Science Association, Chicago, Illinois, 1978; M. Fiedler, "The Participation of Women in American Politics." Prepared for the Annual Meeting of the American Political Science Association, San Francisco, California, 1975; Mezey, "Does Sex Make a Difference"; and Susan Mezey, "Women and Representation: The Case of Hawaii," Journal of Politics, forthcoming, 1978.
    13Mezey, "Does Sex Make a Difference."
    14Diamond, Sex Roles in the State House; F. Gehlen, "Women in Congress," Transaction 6 (October 1969): 36-40; and Kirkpatrick, Political Woman.
    15Kirkpatrick, Political Woman.
    16Kent Jennings and Norman Thomas, "Men and Women in Party Elites: Social Roles and Political Resources," Midwest Journal of Political Science 12 (November 1968): 469-492; and Costantini and Craik, "Women as Politicians."
    17Emmy Werner and Louise M. Bachtold, "Personality Characteristics of Women in American Politics," in Jane Jaquette, ed., Women in Politics (New York: John Wiley, 1974), p. 82.
    18Ibid.
    19James Barber, The Lawmakers (New Haven: Yale University Press, 1965).
    20Hanna F. Pitkin, The Concept of Representation (Berkeley: University of California Press, 1967).

COMMISSIONS ON THE STATUS OF WOMEN
AND BUILDING A LOCAL POLICY AGENDA

Debra W. Stewart

> "He who determines what politics is about runs
> the country, because the definition of alternatives
> is the choice of conflicts, and the choice of con-
> flicts allocates power."[1]

Few would dispute the truth of Schattschneider's
characterization of American politics. Most would agree
that for much of American political history politics has not
been about women's policy concerns. When considered in
tandem, these observations present a compelling rationale
for studying the participation of women in politics from an
agenda-setting perspective.

The virtue of agenda setting as a conceptual lens
emerges clearly in the case of female political participation
at the local level. Though policy of vital concern to women
is resolved by public and private community institutions,
the lion's share of scholarly attention is directed toward
women's participation at the mass level or toward elite female involvement in the more removed state and national
arenas.[2] The elite research that does focus on women as
local-office holders suggests that when in these roles women
do not see themselves as advocates of a women's agenda.[3]

198

Historically, the major vehicle for nonpartisan female political activism in communities, the League of Women Voters   has shunned anything resembling a women's agenda. [4]

    The one institution that in recent years has embraced
this task at the community level is the local Commission on
the Status of Women (CSW).   Existing now in 150 communities across the United States as official advisory boards to
general-jurisdiction governments, CSW are designed to facilitate the building of a women's-issue agenda in their respective communities.

    While focusing on the CSW as the primary unit of
analysis, this article explores two questions: first, what
is gained by viewing the CSW as an agenda-building institution? and second, what is the nature of the policy agenda
such institutions promote?   Elaboration of the agenda-building concept provides the groundwork for full examination of
these questions.

The Concept of Agenda Building

    The specificity with which agenda building is defined
varies greatly in the literature.   In its most inclusive form,
the study of agenda building is defined by Hoppe as "the
analysis of how problems developed, how they were defined,
the courses of action formulated to act on those problems,
the legitimation of one course of action over another, the
emergence of policy systems designed to act on such problems on a continuing basis."[5]   Clearly, agenda building so
conceived is simply everything that politics is about.   On
the other hand, in its most restricted and specific form,
agenda building means simply directing the attention of political decision makers to specific issues.   As Cobb and
Elder develop this definition, the restricted nature of the
range of issues any polity can consider assumes central
importance. [6]   The restriction arises from two sources.

> The first is a systems imperative and is pre-
> dicated on the fact that the processing and atten-
> tion capabilities of any human organization are
> necessarily limited.   The second source of re-
> striction arises from the fact that "all forms of
> political organization have a bias in favor of the
> exploitation of some kinds of conflict and the sup-
> pression of others because organization is the
> mobilization of bias."[7]

Findings of both Crenson and Walker buttress this perspective on the impact of agenda setting.   Crenson argues that
"a community that commits itself to the consideration of
one local concern may, in effect, commit itself to a whole
chain of rationally related issues and diminish its ability to
consider rationally antagonistic issues."[8]   Walker concurs
that focus on a particular issue impacts on future alliances
that are likely to be formed.[9]

Thus attention of decision makers is not the only aspect of agenda building worthy of consideration.   The kinds
of alliances in existence also bear on agenda building activities.   As Cobb and Elder note, if the initial state of
affairs in a conflict were determinate, most issues would
never gain placement on a government agenda, for the strongest side would always succeed in restricting access and in
maintaining the status quo.[10]   But in order to get an issue
on the policy agenda, one side or the other must broaden
its support by altering existing cleavage lines.   Schattschneider talks about this process as "redefinition."[11]

Thus the key questions of agenda building, when
viewed from the perspective of the newly mobilized interests, are these.   How does one gain access to the political
agenda, and who participates in this process?   Once interests in the community at large have defined certain matters
as salient, how do those "matters" translate into "issues"
on the political agenda?   Cobb and Elder frame this question in terms of the gap between the systemic agenda, i.e.,
"a general set of political controversies that will be viewed
at any point in time as falling within a range of legitimate
concerns meriting the attention of policy," and the institutional agenda, i.e., "a set of concrete, specific items sched-
uled for active and serious consideration by a particular institutional decision-making body."[12]

Commissions as Agenda Builders

Viewing Commissions on the Status of Women as
agenda building institutions provides a conceptual framework
within which their activities can be described and assessed.
They are institutions conceived in order to introduce a new
bias into the local political system in which they operate.
As institutions, they are premised on the conviction that
any policy system in which government plays a totally passive role in agenda setting implicitly favors the existing

distribution of resources, including access points. CSW
reflect a general movement, evident at the local level in
the late 1960s and through the 1970s, for local government
to establish institutions for the explicit purpose of helping
groups articulate their problems. [13]

     In Cobb and Elder's terminology Commissions on the
Status of Women can be seen as institutions that bridge the
gap between the systemic women's agenda in the community
and the institutional agenda. Commissions are thus issue
brokers, of a kind, that endeavor to place new problems
relating to women on the formal docket of the local decision-
making bodies. [14] Viewing CSW as agenda-building institutions gives a narrowed and sharpened focus to the analysis
of this effort to institutionalize female participation at the
local level. The institutional raison d'être becomes to en-
lighten policy-making officials on women's policy issues and
to force at least a recognition of the problems issues represent. [15] Agenda building as a conceptual framework makes
no assumption about the outcome of local governmental action on issues placed by the CSW on the formal agenda.

     Some will undoubtedly argue with what may appear
to be a nonresult model for framing discussion of Commissions on the Status of Women. Yet it is appropriate in this
case because the very possibility of gaining the docket remains problematic for many women's issues. The likely
source of this uncertain future for many issues is that the
formal agenda is "restricted by prevailing popular sentiment
as to what constitutes appropriate matters for governmental
action."[16] Historically, the private or domestic domain has
been off-limits to local government. Still, issues most in-
timately impinging on a woman's life chances emanate from
this domain--spouse abuse, child care, abortion, to mention
but a few.[17] As citizen advisory boards, ostensibly selected to ensure broad representation and a balanced view of
community women's interests,[18] CSW have potential to con-
fer legitimacy as a prerequisite for formal agenda status.
Given the private character of many issues we view as wom-
en's policy issues, working with the agenda-building concept
affords the opportunity to examine the activities of Commissions on the Status of Women in what may be one of the
most important roles any women's organization can play in
community politics.

     If agenda building is a conceptual focus worth adopt-
ing, and if Commissions on the Status of Women are the

principal institutions established to carry out the agenda-building process, multiple dimensions of agenda-building activity of Commissions merit examination. The data base supporting this examination will now be elaborated.

Data Base

The data on CSW agenda building were collected as part of a larger study investigating multiple aspects of CSW performance. The nature of local CSW agenda was drawn from a survey of local government Commissions on the Status of Women. Issue-involvement data were coded directly from questionnaires, sent by the Women's Bureau (U. S. Department of Labor) to all Commissions operating during the summer of 1975, asking them to list the major issues with which they were concerned. Officially, there were seventy-five local Commissions at that time.[19] About sixty of these maintained some level of activity; forty-eight of these functioning Commissions returned the questionnaire. In order to gain insight into sources of agenda variation, additional information on the political and demographic setting of each responding commission was drawn from The City-County Data Book: 1972, The State and Local Governmental Special Studies: U.S. Census Bureau, and The Municipal Yearbook, 1973.

The Nature of CSW Issue Agenda Across Communities

Understanding the shape of the issue agenda presented by CSW requires attention to the dynamics of issue expansion. As Cobb and Elder put it, "The underlying proposition is that the greater the size of the audience to which an issue can be enlarged, the greater the likelihood that it will attain systemic agenda standing and thus acceptance to a formal agenda."[20] More specifically, they note, "Issues are likely to be expanded to a larger public if they can be defined broadly to appeal to more subgroups within the populace."[21]

Assuming that Commissions on the Status of Women are responding to a systemic agenda in playing this broker role, we would expect issue placement to occur in the following form. First, issues should appear on CSW agendas with varying frequency, with those issues having the broadest subgroup appeal gaining placement most often. Second, issues reflecting a narrow appeal should cluster together in sets that invite support from a variety of subgroups. Issue clusters might reflect inherently similar problems, or they might suggest a set of conditions jointly produced by a single factor or set of factors in the context within which the Commissions adopting these clusters operate. Here we will explore these expectations derived from agenda-building theory by, first, presenting a rank ordering of CSW agenda items by frequency of occurrence, second, presenting a display of the issue clusters, and third, discussing those clusters in light of the alternative bases for their common agenda placement. Table 1 presents a rank ordering of issues according to frequency of agenda placement based on the 1975 survey of all local Commissions on the Status of Women.

Table 1

Issues on Local CSW Agenda
by Rank Order and Frequency

Rank	Issue	Frequency
1	Employment	24
2	Education	24
3	Rape	14
4	Child Care	13
5	Affirmative Action	12
6	ERA	11
7	Credit	10
8	Legislation State/Federal	9
9	Health	6
10	Women's Rights in Families	5
11	Sexism in Schools	4
11	Reproduction/Population	3
11	Female Offenders	3
12	Media	3
12	Insurance	2
12	Aging	2
12	Economic Status	2
12	Abortion	2
12	Housing	2
12	Miscellaneous Non-Women's Issues	2
12	Abused women	2
13	Child support	1

Clearly, issues do appear on CSW agenda with varying degrees of frequency. Education and employment occur on
the agenda of the commissions surveyed nearly twice as
often as the next most frequently named issues. Both education and employment are goods that most people have
come to expect as a matter of course in modern society,
and equal opportunity in these areas may simply be a value
with which few would disagree.[22] Most of the issues falling in the lower third of the ranking tend to be directed
toward meeting needs of specific subgroups: older women,
abused women, low-income women, etc. Accordingly, the
ease of issue-expansion factor, highlighted by the agenda-
building theory, proves useful in interpreting the skewed
distribution of issues this sample of CSW espoused.

     As Table 1 reveals, most issues do not occur with
the frequency of education and employment. How do these
other issues gain the docket? Agenda theory would suggest
that issues might appear in clusters of some kind. Table
2 presents the results of a factor analysis revealing the
propensity of CSW to adopt clusters of issues. Factor analysis is especially useful in this context, for it isolates in-
terdependencies among issues and attempts to express the
common dimensions underlying the issues in terms of a
smaller number of factors. The figures presented in Table
2, e.g., Economic Status (.90), are factor loadings and are
measures of the degree to which each issue correlates with
the underlying factor. Through examining the correlations
of the factors with the issues it is possible to describe the
dimension measured by each factor. In other words, by
considering both the issues that "load" on each factor and
the strength of these relationships it is possible to "name"
the dimensions extracted from the twenty-one issues in this
factor analysis. The nine factors are listed, in the order
in which they were extracted, in Table 2.

     The data suggest that commissions do adopt clusters
of issues, a finding generally consistent with the expectation
from agenda-building theory that issues must appeal to broad
publics. Coalitions of subgroups constitute a sufficiently
broad public to gain formal agenda status for their collective
interests. The broader question about the structure of issue
clusters--Do clusters contain issues relating to the same
substantive problem, or are they different problems that
share similar causes?--cannot be answered conclusively
through analysis of these 1975 data. Still, in an exploratory
research vein, the clusterings support some rich and potentially fruitful speculation.

Table 2

Issue Clusters*

1) Economic Survival
   1) Economic Status (.90)
   2) Child Support (.89)
   3) Abortion Access (.90)

2) Youth
   1) Sexism in Schools (.74)
   2) Reproduction/Birth
      Control (.87)

3) Government Programs
   1) Education (.67)
   2) Health (.84)
   3) State and Federal
      Legislation (.54)

4) Female Independence
   1) Women's Rights in
      Families (.85)
   2) Insurance (.81)

5) Pure Women's Rights
   1) ERA (.89)
   2) Employment (-.63)

6) Non-Women Specific
   1) Housing (.69)
   2) Miscellaneous (.89)

7) Protection and Care
   1) Child Care (.56)
   2) Rape (.61)
   3) Aging (.64)
   4) Media (.69)
   5) Abused Women
      (.62)

8) Absence of Concern
   with Credit Issues
   (-.90)

9) Absence of Response
   to Federal Initiative
   1) Affirmative Ac-
      tion (-.62)
   2) Status of Female
      Offenders
      (-.79)

*All twenty-one issues have a loading on each factor, but only the issues with the highest loadings are used in identifying a factor. A factor loading of .50 or greater was chosen as the cut-off point for inclusion of an issue in a factor. An orthogonal rotation, varimax, was used to extract the factors from the correlation matrix. For a factor to be included in Table 2, it had to have an eigenvalue of 1 (this statistic measures the amount of variance explained by a single factor). The total variance in the unaltered correlation matrix explained by the nine factors is 79%. The statistical program used was Anthony S. Barr et al., Statistical Analysis System (Raleigh, N.C.: SAS Institute, Inc., 1976), pp. 112-119.

As noted above, issues may be placed together on a CSW agenda because they deal with the same underlying problem that various subgroups might experience in different

forms.   On the other hand, a cluster may be characterized
by a mix of issues dealing with different types of problems,
but possibly reflecting a single set of conditions in the environment within which the agendas are set.   This analysis
permits speculation in both directions.   Factors 1, 3, 4,
5, 7, and 8 lend themselves to the first rationale for issue
clusters.   The issues composing these factors consist of
common substantive themes.   Factor 1, economic status of
low-income women, child support, and abortion (in 1975,
after the 1973 Supreme Court decision), deals with the
problem of economic survival for women living in poverty
or near-poverty.   These issues do not name programs or
policies, but rather suggest needs.   Jointly, they may be
classified as survival issues for poor women.   In Factor 3,
the issues relate to programmatic activities of the government.   Factor 4, including a general concern for women's
rights and the family, and the need for improved insurance
programs for women, suggests a shared substantive theme
relating to the importance of female independence.   Factor
5 embodies a pure concern with the principle of women's
rights, independent of the material payoff in terms of employment opportunity that the ERA will bring.   The common
substantive theme shared by the collection of issues in Factor 7 (with the possible exception of the media) is the need
to secure protection for people who are in a vulnerable or
powerless situation.   Factor 8, representing only the absence of concern with credit, obviously embodies that sole
substantive theme.   In three of the factors, 2, 6, 9, a
single thread is less readily apparent, though even here
some common substantive themes may be worth pursuing
in future research.   Factor 2 may reflect a common concern with the needs and problems of young women.   Factor
6 may reflect a stress by a CSW on issues not relating
directly to women.   Factor 9 may suggest a common un-
willingness to respond to issues stimulated by the federal
initiative, reflected in both affirmative action programs and
programs for female offenders.

    The alternative mode of examining issue clusters
hypothesizes that the basis of clustering of issues resides
in elements of the political, socioeconomic, or organizational context within which these issues gain docket status.   Table 3 lists a set of variables, drawn from the community
politics literature, that might impact on the likelihood of a
commission's placing a cluster of issues on its agenda.
Significant correlations of these variables with factor scores
for commissions simply suggest hypotheses for future re-

search.   Discussion will focus on Factors 2, 6, and 9,
those factors resisting easy interpretation in terms of their
central substantive themes.

    The clustering in Factor 2, correlated as it is with
the level of local unemployment, may reflect a concern in
the broader community about the condition of youth.   The
significance of this youth problem may be magnified for
the Commission on the Status of Women because commissions high on this factor tend to be located in Human Relations Commissions, which are typically charged with concern for a variety of disadvantaged groups in a community.
It is interesting to note that the proportion of youth membership on the commission appears negatively correlated
with this factor, lending credence to the interpretation that
the problems are not inherently similar, but rather that
they reflect a broader contextual condition.   The positive
correlation between Factor VI and the existence of an executive director on the one hand, and a nonpartisan electoral
system on the other, suggests another potentially significant
set of contextual conditions.   A nonpartisan electoral system, with its de-emphasis on responding to organized interests in the community, may foster CSW adoption of agenda-
building strategies that include placing issues not specific
to women on the institutional docket.   This may be a particularly conscious strategy where the commission employs
an executive director who, from her broader perspective,
perceives the value such tangential issues may have in
terms of securing support for pure women's issues within
the context of the reformed political system.   On Factor 9
there are no significant relationships between the absence
of support for these two issues and any of the context variables listed in Table 3.   Thus the substantive interpretation, that these issues reflect an absence of positive response to federal initiative, remains the only apparent interpretation for the cluster.

    This discussion suggests ways we may continue to
look at the basis for the clustering of issues that occurs
on local CSW agenda.   Obviously, future work in this area
would need to probe hypotheses gleaned from such exploratory work.   But whatever the basis of issue clustering may
be, the rationale, from an agenda-building perspective, for
putting issues together remains constant.   The clustering
phenomenon suggests that CSW do carry specific groups of
issues on their agenda and that all issues are not equally
compatible even within the narrow area of women's policy

Table 3.   Issue Clusters Correlated[1] with Political, Socioeconomic,

| | | Issue Clusters | | |
	Source of Variation	Factor 1 Economic Survival . . . . Economic Status/Child Support/ Abortion	Factor 2 (Youth) . . . . Sexism in Schools/ Reproduction- Population	Factor 3 Government Programs . . . . Education/ Health/ Legislation: State-Federal
Political Traits:	Political Culture	-.30*	-.04	-.26
	Reform (% non-partisan)c	.11	-.14	.11
	Form of Electionb	.14	-.07	.02
	Jurisdiction	-.12	.07	.23
	Manager Governmentc	.13	.14	33*
Socio-Economic Traits:	% Unemployed in Civilian Labor Forcea	-.03	.31*	.19
	% Foreign Populationa	-.07	.02	-.15
	% Nonwhitea	.07	.27	-.10
	%Female Head of Householda	.25	.22	-.07
	% Families Below Poverty Levela	.16	.26	.27
	Size of Communitya	-.35*	.05	-.41
Internal Organizational Traits:	Size of Membership	-.09	.08	.05
	Location in Government	.05	.29*	-.23
	Executive Director	.16	-.01	.44*
	Tenure	-.07	-.10	.11
	Advocacy	.25*	.21	-.01
	Minority Membership	-.08	.11	-.02
	Employed Membership	-.13	.04	.31*
	Youth Membership	-.03	-.42*	-.06
	Male Membership	.06	.00	-.06

[1]Pearson's r significant at .08 level marked by*.   Spearman's rank-order correlation (rho) used for Political Culture and Location in Government.

[2]Sources: (a) City-County Data Book, 1972;
            (b) State and Local Government, Special Studies #68, Table 5,
                 U.S. Bureau of Census;
            (c) Municipal Year Book, 1973,

and Organizational Traits of the CSW Agenda-Setting Context[2,3]

Factor 4 Female Independence	Issue Clusters Factor 5 Pure Women's Rights	Factor 6 (Non-Women specific)
. . . .	. . . .	. . . .
Women's Rights in Families/ Insurance	Employment/ ERA	Housing/ Miscellaneous
.16	-.01	.003
-.05	-.04	.36*
-.15	.23	-.17
-.10	.18	-.21
.00	-.06	.25
-.07	.25	-.01
-.03	-.36*	.23
-.38*	-.31*	-.13
-.42*	-.23	-.14
-.15	-.43*	.05
-.30*	-.28	.11
.05	-.22	.00
.27	.01	.04
.16	-.04	.48*
-.17	.20	.17
-.05	.24	.01
-.25	-.03	.17
-.06	-.29	.03
-.04	.19	-.33*
.03	.06	-.03

[3]Supporting literature and operational measures (when not apparent):
(1) Political Culture (commission communities are coded on a 1 to
6 scale with 1=moralistic, 2=predominantly moralistic, 3=somewhat
moralistic, 4=individualistic, 5=predominantly or somewhat individual-

Table 3 continued.

Factor 7 Protection and Care .... Aging/Child Care/Rape/ Media/Welfare	Issue Clusters Factor 8 Absence of Concern with Credit Issues .... Credit	Factor 9 (Absence of Response to Federal Initiative) .... Affirmative Action/Female Offenders
-.00	.10	.00
.32*	.00	-.20
-.26		.08
-.16	-.11	.10
-.11	-.08	-.09
-.05	.02	.10
-.34*	.09	.32*
-.13	.12	-.15
-.21	.06	.18
.01	-.06	-.03
-.28*	-.05	-.13
.36*	.04	.12
.07	-.18	-.05
.14	.04	.11
-.15	.26	-.02
.30*	-.14	-.06
-.04	-.10	.03
-.21	-.12	.05
.08	-.18	-.22
.13	-.03	-.26

istic, and 6=traditional), see Daniel Elazar, American Federalism: A View from the States (2nd ed.; New York: Thomas Y. Crowell Co., 1972); pp. 106-107; (2) Reform (percentage nonpartisan), see Michael Aiken and Robert R. Alford, "Community Structure and Innovation: The Case of Urban Renewal," American Sociological Review, XXXV (August 1970), pp. 650-665; (3) Form of Election (percentage exclusively at

concerns. This finding lends credence to the assertion of
agenda-building theorists that, by focusing attention on one
issue you indirectly influence the kinds of alliances that are
formed[23] and thus the kinds of other issues that can receive
simultaneous agenda status.

Conclusion

        This paper argues that agenda-building theory pro-
vides a useful framework for the analysis of women and
local politics and, more specifically, for the study of local
Commissions on the Status of Women. In conclusion, we
are left with some answers and some new questions.

        Through taking up this agenda-building lens, we have
seen that Commissions on the Status of Women adopt issues
in a predictable fashion. The survey of forty-eight commissions revealed that commissions generally stress a few
issues with broad appeal and that they tend to adopt clusters
of less-generally-attractive issues, thus enhancing the possibility of agenda placement for any one issue in the cluster.
Yet the basis for these clusters in terms of the relative importance of the substantive issue similarity versus conditions
operative in the context within which the agenda is set remains a topic for future study.

        Though such modest conclusions seem to stimulate
yet more questions, answers to these questions promise to

---

large), see Aiken and Alford, "...The Case of Urban Renewal," pp. 650-665; (4) Jurisdiction (percentage city); (5) Manager Form of Government; Socioeconomic Traits, for a review of this literature see Richard I. Hofferbert, "State and
Community Policy Studies: A Review of Comparative Input-
Output Analysis," in James A. Robinson, ed., 3rd Political
Science Annual (Indianapolis: Bobbs-Merrill, 1972); Organizational Traits, for a review of this literature see, James
Q. Wilson, Political Organizations (New York: Basic Books,
1973), pp. 195-260.

provide deeper insight into local-level agenda building in
the women's-policy sphere. Following such questions leads
us one step further toward understanding the core of politics outlined by Schattschneider when he highlighted the relationship between the definition of alternatives, the choice
of conflicts, and the allocation of power.

Notes

     [1]Elmer E. Schattschneider, The Semi-Sovereign Peo-
ple (New York: Holt, Rinehart and Winston, 1960), p. 68.
Emphasis mine.
     [2]For women's political participation at mass level,
see Jo Freemen, The Politics of Women's Liberation (New
York: David McKay, 1975); and Kirsten Amundson, A New
Look at the Silenced Majority (Englewood Cliffs, N.J.: Pren-
tice-Hall, 1976). For research on female elites, see Jeane
Kirkpatrick, Political Woman (New York: Basic Books,
1977); Irene Diamond, Sex Roles in the State House (New
Haven: Yale University Press, 1977); and Women in the
Courts (National Center for State Courts, 1978).
     [3]See Susan Mezey, "Women Politicians and Women's
Issues: The Case of Hawaii." Paper presented at the Amer-
ican Political Science Association Convention, Chicago, Illinois, September 2-5, 1976; and Susan Mezey, "Local Representatives in Connecticut: Sex Differences in Attitudes
Towards Women's Rights Policy." Paper presented at the
American Political Science Association Convention, Washington, D.C., September 1-4, 1977.
     [4]See Martin Gruberg, Women in American Politics
(Oshkosh, Wis.: Academia Press, 1968). Since 1973 the
LWV has been working for ratification of the ERA and during the 1978 convention considered adopting abortion rights
as an issue. Thus there are indications of movement in
the organization toward a stronger commitment to a "wom-
en's agenda."
     [5]Layne D. Hoppe, "Agenda-Setting Strategies: Pollu-
tion Policy" (unpublished Ph.D. dissertation, University of
Arizona, 1969), p. 2, cited in Charles O. Jones, An Introduction to the Study of Public Policy, 2nd ed. (Belmont, Calif.: Wadsworth, 1977), p. 39.
     [6]Roger W. Cobb and Charles D. Elder, Participation
in American Politics: The Dynamics of Agenda-Building
(Baltimore: Johns Hopkins University Press, 1972), p. 10.
     [7]Ibid.
     [8]Matthew Crenson, The Un-Politics of Air Pollution
(Baltimore: Johns Hopkins University Press, 1971), p. 192.

213   CSW and Local Policy Agenda

9Jack L. Walker, "Setting the Agenda in the U.S. Senate: A Theory of Problem Selection," British Journal of Political Science 7, 4 (October 1977), 423-445.
10Cobb and Elder, Participation in American Politics, p. 44.
11Ibid.
12Ibid., p. 10.
13For a clear discussion of the relationship between bias and agenda setting, see Jones, An Introduction to the Study of Public Policy, p. 38.
14Walker has developed a typology of Senate agenda items based on the routineness of their occurrence, with the most routine being the periodically recurring problems and the nonroutine being chosen problems. Walker labels these latter types of issues discretionary agenda items. The CSW agenda is primarily a discretionary agenda. Indeed, some issues that gain placement, such as education, are recurring in a general programmatic sense; but the particular aspect of education addressed in the CSW agenda item is typically nonrecurring. Limited access to athletic programming for high-school women is a discretionary issue on which a commission will focus for a year, or two or even three, but with the explicit intent of resolving the problem so that it will not be recurring. For typology, see Walker, "Setting the Agenda," p. 424.
15Cobb and Elder represent this "recognition of issues" perspective on agenda building; see Cobb and Elder, Participation in American Politics, p. 152.
16Cobb and Elder, Participation in American Politics, p. 93.
17For a discussion of many "private" issues taken as given but actually reflecting public policy see Alvin Schorr, "Family Values and Public Policy" Journal of Social Policy, 1, 1: p. 39.
18For an in-depth discussion of the significance of the balance factor on Commissions on the Status of Women, see Debra W. Stewart, "Local Commissions on the Status of Women: An Examination of their Representative Function." Paper prepared for delivery at the Annual Meeting of the Midwest Political Science Association, Chicago, Illinois, April 20-22, 1978.
19Nongovernment Commissions on the Status of Women were not included in this study because of the variety of shapes and forms they assume. Four such local commissions were registered with the Women's Bureau in 1973-1974. Undoubtedly many more operate in communities across the country.

20Cobb and Elder, Participation in American Politics, p. 110.

21Cobb and Elder present four more specific propositions linking issue characteristics to issue expansion. Examination of these additional propositions is not possible with the data analyzed here; greater knowledge of the community context in which the issue emerged would be required. See Cobb and Elder, Participation in American Politics, pp. 112-124.

22Broad support for some degree of equal treatment in employment has been operative for many years. A Gallup poll reported in 1954 that a solid majority of the population supported equal pay for working women. National legislation passed in the sixties and seventies, prohibiting race/sex discrimination in employment and education, further legitimized these issues. By 1976 a Gallup poll reported 68 percent of those interviewed in a national sample approved of working wives. Equal treatment in education and employment is fundamental to achievement in the work role. Even working-class women, often thought to be estranged from the women's movement, are reported to be attracted to the equal rights in employment and education aspects of the movement ideology. See Kathleen McCourt, Working Class Women and Grass-Roots Politics (Bloomington: Indiana University Press, 1977); and Maren L. Carden, The New Feminist Movement (New York: Russell Sage Foundation, 1974).

23Jack L. Walker, "Setting the Agenda," p. 445.

CONCLUSION

The research reported in this volume stems from a commitment made by the Center for the American Woman and Politics to promote a greater understanding of women's roles in local political systems. Announcing the 1976 Florence Eagleton Grants Program, the Center stressed that, "beyond the simple fact of low representation in local government, little is known about the ways in which women may influence or participate in decision-making for their communities, the barriers to participation that may exist, the difference between men and women in the manner and form of participation, or the variations in the nature of women's public activities in different kinds of communities." The preceding articles aim to narrow that knowledge gap.

From a practical political perspective, research in this direction merits special attention for at least two reasons. First, at the local level, political women are on the move as never before: by 1977 the increase in female local-office holding was at least 36 percent above 1979, and local Commissions on the Status of Women mushroomed from seventy-five in 1975 to 150 in 1977. Second, the inclusion of more women in elected and appointed public offices at all levels of government is a cornerstone of contemporary feminist policy. From a feminist perspective, women in public office are not only a symbol of power and influence within the system but also an asset in implementing a women's policy agenda. Hence special expectations are placed on new female entrants into the political system.

In approaching these practical and theoretical corners,
contributors to this volume have drawn on the theory and
concepts of political science as well as social psychology
and organization theory. The ordering framework adopted
is simply sequential: how do women attain public office?
(Selection and Recruitment) and how do they perform once
in that public role? (Policy Positions and Organizational
Roles). Though the research reported here offers only ten-
tative answers to these questions, the insights provided hold
significant implications for both current theory and the future research agenda.

Selection and Recruitment

    In the selection and recruitment of women to local
public office a deeper and broader understanding has been
achieved, particularly regarding distaff recruitment avenues,
barriers to entry, and ambition.

    Recruitment Avenues. A number of studies looking
at women officeholders across the American political system
show that women achieving public office follow routes into
office that differ from those typical for men.[1] The 1977
Eagleton survey of women officeholders nationwide reports
that, while intensive party experience is typically in the
background of women in public office, they feel that men
have tried to exclude them from leadership roles. The
fact, established in the Eagleton survey, that women's past
public-office holding is more likely to have been appointive
and men's more likely to have been elective buttresses this
point. The difference "may be an indirect indicator of a
tendency for party organization to reward party service by
women with minor appointive offices in place of nomination
for elective office."[2]

    The findings reported in Part I of this volume suggest
that while support is forthcoming for the differential-treat-
ment thesis, the ultimate routes taken by men and women
at the local level look much alike. Margolis tells us that
family roles inevitably creep into party activity to shape the
experience of party involvement differently for men and wom-
en. For women involved in party work Margolis found that
gaining self-esteem comes from completing tasks in an invisible fashion. Thus the "better" women do their jobs, the
less likely they are to be tapped for elective office. In other
words, party service may neither mean the same thing nor

yield the same results for men and women. Findings such
as these inevitably raise questions about alternative organizational settings for launching female public-office holding
careers. Perhaps organizations where women lay strong
claim to experience, like the PTA, or where they constitute
nearly the entire membership, like the League of Women
Voters, provide more effective launching pads than do political parties. Here the impact of family roles is diminished
by the weight of "expertise" or by the absence of the counterparts to the dependent women--the strong male.

Merritt's study of suburban Chicago officeholders provides explicit information about organizational backgrounds
and thus sheds some light on this issue. When asked about
involvement in a variety of community-based organizations,
men and women indicated that they were equally active in
four civic organizations prior to election--with half of the
sample being involved in a partisan or nonpartisan political
group. The women, however, were also disproportionately
involved in both the LWV (51 percent to 2 percent) and PTA
(65 percent to 33 percent). This might suggest that experience outside the conventional male feeder organizations may
be a prerequisite for some women who ultimately gain public office. Still, party involvement remains a significant
background factor in the careers of many political women.

In the Mezey study, party is clearly the key to recruitment to local office for the Connecticut women. Mezey
does find that the women in her sample more frequently engaged in the routine tasks of political activism. Nonetheless, it is by paying dues to the local party organization
that women move into public roles in their community.

These local-level studies spotlight several questions
for future researchers. Are party organizations the most
efficient route to office holding for women or rather are the
dues exacted from female members too great? How effective are other civic organizations as training grounds for
political women? What kind of outside organizational or
social resources might be necessary for women to compensate for their relative disadvantage on male-dominated recruiting grounds?

Barriers to Entry. The political-science literature
offers several explanations for why women are underrepresented in the ranks of public officials. The three principal
explanations currently espoused label as causal factors:

political socialization, situational/structural conditions, and/
or active discrimination.   The political-socialization explanation suggests that politics is a man's game in which female strengths cannot be effectively utilized.   The situational/
structural argument, labeled by Welsh the "sex role argument," has two components: situation (women as homemakers don't have time, energy, or contacts necessary to
pursue a political career) and structural condition (women
have been socialized not to pursue the male occupations,
such as business, law, and other professions from which
officeholders are chosen).[3]   The discrimination explanation
suggests that either party leadership or the electorate choos-
es to deny leadership roles to distaff aspirants simply because of their sex.   As both Mezey and Welsh have suggested elsewhere, these explanations should not be viewed
as mutually exclusive.   On the contrary, they may be working together in a reinforcing pattern.

       The research reported in Part I provides mixed sup-
port and nonsupport for this set of explanations.   Officeholders in the Mezey and Merritt studies fail to exhibit
many of the differences that are thought to exist between
male and female politicos and to work a special burden on
women.   Mezey, for example, finds virtually no difference
between men and women Connecticut officials in terms of
their structural condition or their early political socialization.   The only difference between males and females was
that the husbands of female officeholders were often involved
in public or party office and wives of male officeholders
were not.   The Merritt study, by contrast, finds some mixed
support for the socialization barrier and clear support for
the structural barrier to entry.   No strong sex differences
were found in motivation for office in Merritt's study.
Among these suburban officeholders motivation for office
defined in terms of achievement, power, or affiliation showed
none of the sex differences that might be expected from the
different socialization men and women receive.   Differences
did emerge in two personality traits: competitiveness and
activist orientation, with women less likely to describe themselves as competitive and more likely to agree that they are
dissatisfied with the world and are trying to change it.   This
finding does fit more comfortably with the "sex makes a difference due to socialization" argument.

       In terms of the family condition of female officehold-
ers--the situational variable--sex clearly does make a difference in their experience.   Among Merritt's suburban office-

holders, women seek political office when their children are
older. Women, as well, see their husbands as supportive
of their political activity. Such spouse support is not evident in the responses of male legislators.

Active discrimination is typically cited as a third
barrier to entry for would-be female officeholders. Empirically tracking a pattern of active discrimination, however, is not an easy task. The difficulties involved as
well as potential conceptual handles for dealing with difficulties in studying active discrimination are highlighted especially in the Mezey and Cook studies. Mezey reports that
the Connecticut women saw no overt prejudice against them
or favoritism toward male candidates either by the electorate or party officials. But Cook's work on the concept of
political culture begins to put this Connecticut finding in
perspective. Defining political culture as "a subset of the
beliefs, values and styles of the general culture, which gives
shape to political structures and behaviors,"[4] Cook finds
that political culture works indirectly through social and
political phenomena to affect opportunities for women in
government. Juxtaposing the findings of Cook and Mezey
regarding this discrimination issue highlights the possibility
that the real experience of women aspirants for local office
in Connecticut may differ radically from that of women in
some other regions of the country and that the difference
may be tied to political culture.

The future research agenda on "barriers to entry"
must therefore focus on larger political factors, like political culture, in an effort to probe these undercurrents
that inform the socialization experience of women, shape
their structural and situational condition, and define norms
that legitimize or discourage discrimination. As well, continued research on how these factors interact at local levels is in order. As Mezey points out, we should beware
of blithely assuming that generalizations at state and national levels apply to local levels as well. In studying the
interaction between these explanatory factors, scholars con-
ducting future research must be sensitive to the unusual
characteristics of the local setting.

Ambition. As the number of female officeholders
grows, increased attention is given to those factors that
may aid in explaining differences among women in terms
of their recruitment-selection experience. Increasingly ambition level comes into focus. The 1977 Eagleton national

survey reports that politically ambitious women differ from
less ambitious officeholders on a variety of dimensions:
they are younger, better educated, receive more encouragement from their husbands, and are more conscious of sex
discrimination.[5] Of the research reported in this volume
only Merritt directly tests ambition in relationship to recruitment and selection, but her results are noteworthy, especially on two points. First, she finds that regarding both
motivation for seeking office and personality differences, sex
fails to differentiate response among the ambitious. Ambitious women simply seem more like men. Second, in terms
of recruitment paths the only variable related to high ambition for women is League of Women Voters membership:
highly ambitious women are less likely to be active in the
League of Women Voters. The first finding supplements
other findings of gender-based difference among officeholders
to suggest that ambition is more significant than sex. The
second finding merits further study in conjunction with Mezey's findings that Connecticut female officeholders experienced
none of the typically reported limitations to advancement.
Perhaps women attracted both to the League of Women Voters and to local office in Connecticut have not only low ambition but also low perception of barriers to advancement,
and these factors may reinforce one another. Perception
of an open road to office holding for women may simply reflect a "false consciousness" susceptible to partial probing
by examination of ambition levels.

       As well, ambition ties into political culture. Clear-
ly, the individualistic culture, with its stress on personal
achievement, might give broader scope to ambitious people--
male or female--while a traditional political culture may define political ambition itself as a male trait. Future work
at all levels of the system, but perhaps especially in local
politics, must take account of ambition. Ambition may
shape both how women interpret their entire political experience as well as the political value they see as inherent
in the local office itself. Doubtless it also will suggest new
hypotheses testable in analyzing the relative value of alternative organizational launching pads for female political
careers. Though no single variable holds the key to
total understanding of the entire recruitment-selection
process, controlling for ambition seems mandatory in
all future studies investigating gender differences among
public officials.

Policy Positions and Organizational Roles

Part II of this volume shifts from recruitment and
selection to consider how women perform after they land a
public office. Obviously, from the perspective of the feminist scholarship in particular, the question of the possibilities for women officeholders advancing a "women's agenda"
assumes particular importance. The research reported in
Part II provides new insights in two important areas: the
impact of gender on political outlook and the role of structure and institutions in channeling and shaping that outlook.

Gender as a Component of Political Outlook. The
conventional wisdom on women officeholders conveys that
gender is a component of political outlook and performance
as well as of political recruitment and mobility. The Eagleton 1977 survey of officeholders nationwide shows women as
ideologically more liberal than men and as holding to feminist positions on such women's issues as ERA, abortion,
social security for homemakers, child care, and the role
of government and industry as ensuring equal rights for
women. Again the Eagleton survey presents them as public servants with a greater concern for constituent relations,
for policy development, and for being well informed on pend-
ing issues than are their male counterparts. 6

In general the studies of women officeholders reported in this volume support the Eagleton survey conclusion
that gender is a component of political outlook and performance. However, these studies of local-office holding also
indicate that consideration of some intervening factors may
be essential to meaningful interpretation of a gender-linked
outlook. In support of the thesis that gender informs outlook, Mezey reports that women politicians in her sample
clearly felt female officeholders should have a special responsibility for attention to concerns and interests of wom-
en in society. A large majority of women believed that political women should take leading positions on women's issues. (Male officeholders were less convinced of this gender-specific responsibility.) But it is noteworthy that there
was no significant relationship between views of "responsibility" for women's issues and feminist ideology. Mezey
stresses that the "women's" interest that Connecticut politicians think women should represent are not necessarily
political in content.

Cook's study of judges provides an opportunity for a

second view of the impact of feminist attitudes and finds a
slightly different relationship.   Here feminism does distinguish between the attitudes of women judges toward their
mission.   Feminists consider sex-discrimination cases more
important than do nonfeminists.   And they would decide simulated cases consistently in favor of the feminist response.
It is also interesting to note that women judges are conscious of institutional constraints and are more favorable
to new social roles for women who demand them then is
the general population.   Even nonfeminists are ahead of
public opinion in this regard.

     Merritt confirms Mezey's finding that gender contrib-
utes significantly to political outlook but finds that if you
look only at employed women many gender differences disappear.   Those differences remaining relate to the role orientation of the officeholders, the perception of citizen trust,
and support for changes in women's public roles.   The dur-
ability of this last gender-linked difference is fairly self-
explanatory.   Women in public roles are predisposed to be
supportive of changes legitimating their incumbency--whatever
their work status.   However, lingering sex difference in role
orientation and perception of citizen trust, even among working women, has no straightforward explanation.   The findings are nonetheless significant.   The fact that even working
women express a preference for "achieving concrete end-
products" and that they also believe the citizens perceive
them as more trustworthy suggests women may continue to
contribute a gender-specific perspective of the political process, irrespective of changing work experience.

     Comparing these findings drawn from different insti-
tutional and geographic settings reveals an important area
for future research.   Continued investigation of the precise
impact of gender on outlook and performance, controlling
for conditions in addition to employment status, is called
for.   Does the nature of the gender-outlook relationship
vary by office or by level of government?   If such variation can be tied to office or level, does the difference simply
reflect a difference in candidate pools, or rather is there
more room for a gender-specific viewpoint in some offices
and less in others?   Finally, when feminist consciousness
emerges in groups of public officials is it directly trans-
lated into policy decision?   In what kinds of policy decisions
does it find early expression?

     Role of Structures and Institutions in Channeling and

Shaping the Outlook of Female Officeholders. Once it is
established that women do infuse politics with a gender-
distinct outlook in some areas and that feminist ideology
does make a difference, attention turns to structural influences. How do institutional structures contribute to the
outlook and behavior of political women? How do women,
especially feminists, channel this outlook once in institutional settings, and how do these settings shape their outlook and options? These questions are new ones in the
study of women and politics, and have thus far received
scant attention. The reasons are obvious. Until relatively
recently there have not been enough female occupants of
public office to study either their institutional experience
or the relationship between the structure and outlook or
action. Some new insights generated by the present research provide sound leads for future research in the area.
Three points merit special note.

        The influence of institutional setting and prescribed
roles on organizational behavior is well established in the
literature. Future research on women in politics should
take careful account of the way institutions and roles channel the outlook of female officeholders. As the Stewart
study of Commission on the Status of Women board-staff
relationships suggests, gender doesn't translate into a single
policy position, even among women uniformly committed to
"women's issues." Differences within gender emerge as a
function of role orientations of commissioners and staff.
The fact of considerable congruence between commissioner
and staff on substantive issues and substantially less congruence between the two groups on functional activities lends
credence to the assertion that the roles these women play
structure their attitudes and outlooks.

        Sex ratio within the political bodies on which women
serve has also been proposed as a factor channeling outlook.
Yet both Cook and Mezey fail to find proportions of women
in official roles as useful in explaining perspectives on wom-
en's roles. Neither the women judges of the Cook study,
nor the municipal officeholders of the Mezey work, reacted
to a sex-skewed ratio in the same manner as officials studied elsewhere in the bureaucratic setting. These findings
hardly justify discarding the proportions theory in analysis
of political women. However, future research in this area
must be sensitive to the fact that political women--unlike
bureaucratic women--come to the organization with substantial independent resources. Thus to the extent that the

theory remains viable in studying officeholders, new indicators for the influence of sex-skewed ratio must be sought.

Finally, once in a position to translate political orientation into a specific policy agenda, institutional constraints act to invite some issues, shun others, and cluster
still others. The Stewart study of Commissions on the Status of Women agenda building substantiates this point. Future research here will need to ask how the different institutions available at the local level shape the expression of
feminist political orientation.

Implications for Political Studies

In aggregate, this research still yields less than con-
clusive answers to all questions raised. Yet what hopefully
does emerge from the coordinated effort reflected here is
both new information about the political women and a more
penetrating insight into her future on the local political
scene. A still more ambitious claim is that the preceeding
articles broaden and deepen our understanding of what political life more generally is all about.[7] This volume concludes with a brief reflection on this larger theme.

Students of American politics, especially observers
of the local political scene, generally acknowledge that opportunity for selection and recruitment is not the same for
everyone in the polity.[8] Local elites are far from a mirror image of the electorate, and historically the new entrant,
differing from incumbents by virtue of a lower social status,[9] seldom receives an invitation to join in the game of
politics. Such an invitation is virtually never extended to
such marginal people when they arrive at the gate in large
numbers. These aspiring but blocked politicos might at
times continue to pursue existing channels; at other times
they take new avenues in search of a crack through which
they can enter. The response of the American political
system to newly conscious political women and to the wom-
en's movement itself illustrates this basic feature.

Political parties, long a standard training ground for
would-be local political elites, typically utilize a highly differentiated role structure that assigns lower status and role
activities to women. Women tapped for higher status activities most closely approximate the male model. It is in
response to such impenetrability that new institutions like

Commissions on the Status of Women are emerging to promote the agenda of the women's movement. Yet even when
new institutions are created, some sharpness of thrust is
inevitably lost as these special bearers of a new agenda attempt to have an impact on and thus mesh with the established decision-making institutions.

Once marginal groups capture a space on the political
scene, government institutions themselves have an inexorable
way of demanding adherence to accepted rules of the game.
While always procedural in content, such rules translate into substantive effect. Often the extent to which existing
rules undercut the original raison d'être turns on the via-
bility of the ideology guiding the new entrant's ascent of office. Whether the focus is on an institution, such as a
Commission on the Status of Women, or on an individual,
like a municipal-office holder or a judge, ideology or political belief system is central. The capacity to make way
for individuals inspired by an ideology that informs thought
and action may be the ultimate test of a local political system's capacity for introducing not only new people but also
new values into the policy-making process. In the final
analysis, an openness to a feminist perspective may be the
touchstone by which the full integration of women into local
politics in America must be judged. In a broader sense,
the political system itself is challenged once again in the
process.

Notes

[1]Marilyn Johnson and Susan Carroll, Profile of Wom-
en Holding Office, II (New Brunswick, N.J.: Center for the
American Woman and Politics-Eagleton Institute of Politics,
1978), p. 56A.
[2]Ibid.
[3]Susan Welch, "Recruitment of Women to Local Office: A Discriminant Analysis," Western Political Quarterly 31, 3 (September 1978), p. 372.
[4]Beverly Cook, "Political Culture and the Selection
of Women Judges in Trial Courts," p. 5.
[5]Johnson and Carroll, Profile of Women Holding Office, p. 57A.
[6]Ibid.
[7]See Melissa A. Butler, "Ideology and Methodology in
the Study of Images of Women in Political Thought." Con-
ference paper delivered at the Annual Meeting of the Southern

Political Science Association, Atlanta, Georgia, November 3-5, 1976, p. 4.

[8]See Kenneth Prewitt, The Recruitment of Political Leaders: A Study of Citizen Participation (Indianapolis: Bobbs-Merrill, 1970).

[9]For a discussion of the treatment of status inferiors, see Joseph M. Berger et al., Status Characteristics and Social Interaction: An Expectation--States Approach (New York: Elsevier, 1977); and Marilyn Johnson and Marsha Lichtenstein, "Perceptions About Women in Politics: An Exploration of the Effects of Female Colleagues on Local Officials." Paper presented at the 1978 Annual Meeting of the American Political Science Association, New York, New York, 1978.

INDEX